SUN~DRENCHED GARDENS

SUN~DRENCHED GARDENS

THE MEDITERRANEAN STYLE

Photography by Lucinda Lewis
Text by Jan Smithen

HARRY N. ABRAMS, INC., PUBLISHERS

NOTE ON CAPITALIZATION

In keeping with current garden writing practice, the word *Mediterranean* when capitalized refers to the Mediterranean Sea and the areas around it. When not capitalized, *mediterranean* refers to a type of climate, the vegetation, and the garden styles found in that climate.

Editor: Elisa Urbanelli
Designer: Dana Sloan
Production Director: Hope Koturo

Library of Congress Cataloging-in-Publication Data

Smithen, Jan.
      Sun-drenched gardens : the Mediterranean style / text by Jan Smithen ;
      photographs by Lucinda Lewis.
      p. cm.
Includes bibliographical references and index.
      ISBN 0-8109-3290-3
      1. Gardens—Mediterranean Region. 2. Mediterranean-type plants.
3. Mediterranean climate. I. Lewis, Lucinda. II. Title.
      SB454.3.M43 S65 2002
      712'.09182'2—dc21

                                        2002002820

Published in 2002 by Harry N. Abrams, Incorporated, New York

Printed and bound in Italy
10 9 8 7 6 5 4 3

Harry N. Abrams, Inc.
100 Fifth Avenue
New York, N.Y. 10011
www.abramsbooks.com

Abrams is a subsidiary of  LA MARTINIÈRE
G R O U P E

Va, pensiero, sull'ali dorate;
Va, ti posa sui clivi, sui colli,
Ove olezzano tepide e molli
L'aure dolci sel suolo natal!

Fly, thought, on wings of gold;
go rest upon the slopes and hills,
where, soft and mild, the sweet air
of our native land lies fragrant!

—Chorus of the Hebrew slaves
Nabucco, by Giuseppe Verdi
Libretto: Temistocle Solera

CONTENTS

INTRODUCTION 8

THE MEDITERRANEAN LOOK 17

ENDLESS SUNSHINE—PRECIOUS WATER 41

LIVING OUTDOORS 71

MEDITERRANEAN STYLE: GARDEN ELEMENTS AND DETAILS 99

GREAT PLANTS, INSPIRED PLANTINGS 147

INDEX 172

GARDENS THAT MAY BE VISITED BY APPOINTMENT 176

SUGGESTED READING AND REFERENCE 176

INTRODUCTION

A harbinger of land arrives with the warm offshore breeze . . . an aromatic blend of dry pine and olives, the slight menthol of cistus and sage, a sharp tang of cypress and cedar, and perhaps the sweet fragrance of citrus and lavender. Long before we see landfall, we sense it. And memory creates a nostalgic painting of our destination . . . the gray-green vegetation among rocky outcroppings, mountains plunging down to the sea, the earthy colors of tiny, walled villages perched among the highest rocks, rolling hills crosshatched with vineyards and terraced with olives, all basking under the hot summer sun. We close our eyes and savor the vision, now replete with that familiar fragrance, sweet, pungent, and slightly resinous.

The garden of the Villa Medici at Fiesole, Italy, looks out over the Arno valley. One of the earliest terraced gardens, it was built in the mid-fifteenth century by sculptor and architect Michelozzo Michelozzi, a master of his time. The garden is perfectly sited into the side of a promontory to take advantage of the cooling breezes during the summer and the warming sun out of the south during the winter. A simplicity of line characterizes both the house and the garden, which never compete with the magnificent view.

The hot, high-pitched colors of bougainvillea have become so identified with the mediterranean style that we likely forget the bougainvillea is a tropical plant. The scorching reds, the screeching purples, the corrosive magentas all look so right in brilliant light, so dramatic against warm-toned houses, gardeners are shocked when the shrubby vine is damaged by frost. If it can be protected and irrigated through its first years, a "bougie" recovers quickly from any later damage and becomes drought tolerant.

This warm scent, these warm colors evoke the Mediterranean region and the Mediterranean garden no matter where in the world we are.

The mediterranean climate is a favored one. Winters are usually mild with intermittent rain, which is often gentle, but can be howling and torrential. Between storms, bright sunny days pull us outside. Springtime is damp and verdant, the hills drizzled with bright color from native wildflowers and bulbs. The four months of summer are moderately hot and totally dry, with day after day of blue sky and bright sunshine.

The typical summer day begins with the first rays of sun streaking from the cloudless horizon. As the sun rises, the sky becomes flat and so brilliant you must hunt for a shady place or find your sunglasses. And the long, hot afternoon engenders a sleepiness in man and beast alike. But this gives way to the promise of dusk and a warm evening spent outside.

Late afternoon is always a special time in a mediterranean garden. It comes with hushed quiet as the sun draws long shadows across the patio, the buzz of cicadas or the call of a bird, the glow of a red leaf as the sun strikes it from behind, the warmth of the evening air against bare arms, and the crunch of dry leaves underfoot releasing that familiar pungent odor. You find yourself lingering there over conversation long into the night.

The mediterranean climate is found in only five major areas of the world: the Mediterranean basin itself, coastal California, parts of southern and western Australia, central coastal Chile, and the southwestern tip of South Africa. The largest area is that of the Mediterranean basin. There, where Western civilization began, man has been practicing the art of gardening for centuries.

Out of the great diversity of Mediterranean history, culture, and religion came the traditions of garden-making that then spread throughout the Western world. It is natural, then, that landscape design and garden elements originating there have been copied, enlarged upon, and reinterpreted down through hundreds of years. They are still found in today's gardens.

Because of the mild, dry weather, people live outdoors in a mediterranean climate more than in other regions. Thus, long ago, garden-makers invented ways of making that outdoor living easier and more comfortable. Problems—such as too much sunshine and not enough water, winds sweeping out of the deserts or mountains, foraging animals, thieving bandits, or prying eyes—all had to be solved. Over the thousands of years since the gardens of Egypt and Mesopotamia, solutions have evolved, been lost and then rediscovered, and even been perfected. These solutions are the models for the modern garden features we see today.

For example, the walled garden turns its delights inward for the enjoyment of only those who live within. As far back as ancient Persia, high walls around the garden were essential for protection and relief from the desert. Down through the centuries, walled garden spaces have been valued for the retreat and privacy they provide. The walled garden is rarely used in the United States because it is thought undemocratic, and some city governments even legislated against it.

▶ Even details can create a mediterranean mood. A small pot of *Echeveria* hybrids softened with ice plant *(Lampranthus deltoides)* echoes the pink walls and milky blue shutters of this country house in southern France.

▲ In vivid contrast to the filmy foliage and gnarled trunks of pepper trees *(Schinus molle)*, variegated *Agave americana* echoes the yellow blooms of wild mustard in the fields beyond. Designed by Julie Heinsheimer, this dry-garden planting creates a mediterranean mood before you even arrive at the home of Mr. and Mrs. Charles Shriver in Palos Verdes, California.

However, the sanctuary of a high-walled garden is still prized in Spain, Italy, Greece, and eastern Mediterranean countries.

Cultural and religious traditions have also determined certain elements of mediterranean garden style. Because of water's scarcity, particularly in the eastern Mediterranean, it has always been treated with particular reverence. The ancient Persians re-created the desert oasis when making their pleasure gardens. These became their symbols of Paradise on earth. Just as the oasis represented relief from desert heat, greenness, and shade from the hot sun, the garden also became a sanctuary.

In Islamic belief, water—its sight, sound, taste, and feel, combined with the walled garden's sense of refuge—represents Paradise as promised by Allah. The four rivers of Paradise specified in the Koran—pure water, milk, wine, and honey—were laid out in these gardens, as if they were rising up out of the center of the earth. They flowed out in four directions, running in rills, or narrow channels. Symbolic of Allah's divine gifts to the faithful, the waterways divided the garden into four square or rectangular quadrants. And this design is the basis of the formal four-part, or quadripartite, garden today. It was taken by the

English yews *(Taxus baccata)*, clipped to pointed cones, echo the peaked shapes of the Italian cypress behind, and the annual red Flanders field poppies *(Papaver rhoeas)* romp underneath every spring. The combination of English and Italian elements is particularly significant in this garden at Villa Chigi Cetinale, whose owner, Lord Lambton, has added plantings in the English style since 1977.

Moors to Spain and Portugal, then by the Spanish and Portuguese conquerors to the New World. Even today, you can still see the quadripartite design in the mission gardens of California.

Shade from the intense summer sun is of prime importance to mediterranean gardens. Always more of a sensory experience than a visual picture, it is as precious as water in a dry climate. In early Roman gardens shade was often created by structures such as arcades, loggias, arbors, and pergolas. But trees and large shrubs were prized by early garden-makers as well. There is evidence on cuneiform tablets that even the ancient Assyrians regarded trees as wartime plunder. After a victory, they would take the trouble to dig out trees and transport them back to their own palace gardens!

Italian Renaissance garden architects, those masters of delight, designed shady bowers where one could sit enclosed, cooled and hidden by greenery, yet be able to survey the garden and all who would walk there. Modern garden designers have inherited so many shade-making devices and techniques to choose from that we all benefit from these centuries of experimentation.

The colors of a mediterranean garden are the colors of the earth, the sky, and the sea. These blues, ochers, and clay colors set off the soft gray-greens, blue-greens, and olive-greens of mediterranean-climate foliage to its best advantage. And modern designers from all over the world use this color palette to evoke a mediterranean mood.

Pots and urns for planting have always been popular in the mediterranean region, where they are made of local clay. A factory for making clay pots on the island of Crete still uses the traditional method of throwing the clay by hand on rotating turntables, and the lovely, pale terra-cotta containers are prized by gardeners as far away as California.

Tightly clipped arches of Italian cypress *(Cupressus sempervirens)* at Clos du Peyronnet serve as a dramatic foil to the surrounding foliage and beckon visitors to investigate what lies at their end.

Natural, unmilled wood and stripped tree branches are frequently used for pergolas and trellises in mediterranean gardens. Their color ages to a soft gray as vines lace up, around, and through the structure, soon obscuring it completely. Walls and paving are made and decorated with local stone and shells, while the very color of the house reflects the color of the earth. All this combines to give the mediterranean garden a vibrant sense of place.

Another fascinating instance of religious and cultural mandates shaping important garden features is the use of decorative tile and wrought-iron filigree. The Islamic religion forbids the representation of living forms to decorate dwellings, furnishings, and even gardens. So the early Arabic garden-makers employed colorful tiles to emulate flower color, and wrought-iron filigree to suggest trees and shrubs. This tradition came to Spain with the conquering Moors. Even today, with the original rationale long forgotten, no Spanish garden is complete without its beautiful tilework and fanciful wrought iron. One finds tile designs and wrought iron in most mediterranean style gardens.

The production of food has always been an important function of mediterranean gardens. Early Persians grew dates, pomegranates, citrus, and figs as edging to their Paradise gardens. Ancient Greeks and Romans grew olives, grapes, and many kinds of stone fruit, both as crops and as ornamentals. As these cultures spread throughout the Mediterranean region, they brought their food plants with them, all the while seeking far and wide for new varieties with better taste or larger fruit. Many of the green, leafy vegetables we enjoy today originated around the northern Mediterranean as wild plants, dug up and brought home to be planted in the kitchen garden. In fact, the Latin word *hortus* first meant an enclosed garden of cultivated greens. It was always located close to the dwelling and worked in by the women of the household, while the men worked in the fields. This food-growing tradition has lingered and today remains a vital part of mediterranean garden style. Growing food plants close to living areas where they are seen, smelled, and perhaps tasted only adds a warm seductiveness to the beauty of the garden.

As culture, religion, and necessity dictated how people lived, a characteristic garden style evolved around the Mediterranean Sea. It is a style we now recognize as fitting to the climate. The other four mediterranean climate zones (California, Western Australia, South Africa, and Chile) are culturally younger societies that were colonized by Europeans who dominated the native populations. The newcomers brought with them garden precepts and customs from home, then attempted to force this model upon their new landscape. Often this has resulted in either failure or excessive and wasteful exploitation of natural resources.

This book seeks to identify and celebrate traditional mediterranean design ideas, to demonstrate how they suit the climate, and to inspire gardeners to appreciate the beauty and practicality of climate-appropriate planting. The mediterranean climate reveals more pleasures than problems, and more delights than disappointments. It is a time-honored aesthetic that is constantly evolving and never goes out of style.

This rustic water feature is composed of a stone water trough and a piece of granite, into which an old water tap and tubing have been inserted through a drilled hole. It gives the impression of a constantly dribbling antique faucet. Behind is an informal hedge of Pacific wax myrtle *(Myrica californica)* with clumps of the gray-leafed perennial *Arctotis acaulis* 'Magenta' on either side. Lemon-scented thyme *(Thymus* 'Pink Ripple') sprawls on the gravel-covered terrace, next to a potted lemon tree.

THE MEDITERRANEAN LOOK

A French *bastide* farm-house was re-created in San Juan Capistrano, California, for Wally and Susie Moore, and garden designer Carole McElwee created an informal mediterranean style garden to fit the lay of the land and echo the style of the house. One approaches the entry from a gravel drive marked with two mature Italian cypress *(Cupressus semper-virens)*, punctuating the sky and setting the mood. A broken concrete walk planted with fragrant creeping thyme *(Thymus serpyllum* 'Pink Chintz'*)* skirts the perfectly clipped hedge of upright rosemary *(Rosmarinus officinalis* 'Blue Spires'*)*, leading one to the door in a cloud of pungent scent.

If we were to be set down in a Mediterranean garden on an early summer's day just as the sun rises, the colors of the garden would be our first impression. Early morning light glows warm as it shines on the earthy hues of stone and plaster that form the walls, paving, and paths. Painted surfaces are most often shades of blue, from pale to dark, but always with a soft, milky quality.

The colors of the garden plants themselves would also disclose just where in the world we were. From trees and shrubs to smaller, more ephemeral plants, the foliage is generally in shades of gray, with myriad undertones all the way from green and blue to rust, and even red. Green foliage has a yellowish cast and the backs of many leaves are coated white with a natural fuzz called *indusium*. All this combines to drape the garden with a soft, shimmering appearance, as if a mantle of the sheerest silk had been thrown over it.

The visual texture of the garden is fine. So many mediterranean-climate plants are needled, or have small leaves, as an adaptation for conserving what moisture is within them. They give the garden a fine-grained look, which is best set off by contrasting them against bold, stark forms. Fine-needled rosemary, tiny-leafed correa, and silvery sand-hill sage *(Artemisia pycnocephala)* accented with the dramatic forms of agave, large aloe, or the huge rosette of *Echeveria agavoides* make telling combinations. Other foils for fine foliage could be interesting rocks, small sculptures, or large terra-cotta pots. A creative way to use a cracked or damaged vessel is to place it within a planting scheme, lending a patina of age to the design.

As the sun rises higher in the sky on the summer's day, we begin to feel the hard, bright light that is common to all mediterranean climes. Pale flower colors fade to white, and white becomes so reflective we must turn away. The hills in the distance become blue with haze, and everyone looks for the relief of cool shade. Shade itself takes on another color, darker and deeper green, cooling to the eyes. As much a feeling as it is something seen, shade is essential to every garden.

We would look for water as well—perhaps a still pond, narrow rill, or dribbling fountain. It does not have to roar, cascade, or even splash, because just the sight or faintest trickle of water prompts a feeling of comfort and relief, as it has for thousands of years.

Afternoon is the moment for those bright, intense flower colors so widely planted in mediterranean gardens. Because the harsh clarity of mediterranean light washes away pale pastels and delicate tints, the eye longs for strong flower color. Fully saturated colors come alive under drench-ing brilliant sunshine: the brilliant reds of callistemons, bougainvillea, or California fuchsia *(Zauschneria californica)*; the glowing orange blooms of pomegranates, many lantanas, or lion's tail *(Leonotis leonurus)*; the intense golden yellows of flannel bush *(Fremontodendron californicum)* or Copper Canyon daisy *(Tagetes lemmonii);* and the vivid violet-blues of Cleveland sage *(Salvia clevelandii)*, S. 'Indigo Spires', or woolly blue curls *(Trichostema lanatum)*.

Now too, the nose begins to sense the defining scent of those aromatic plants that grow so well in this climate. As the heat of the day releases the fragrant oils contained in their leaves, these plants add another dimension to the garden, beyond their good looks. These are not the sweet perfumes of flowers, but leaf smells; pungent, spicy, menthol, nose-wrinkling smells, thought by botanists to be a protective adaptation against grazing animals. Plants such as rosemary, rockrose, Cleveland sage, santolinas, artemisias, nepetas, and even cypress, myrtle, and lavender beg to be crushed between fingers and held to the nose. The small, enclosed courtyards so typical of the mediterranean garden concentrate these heady waves of scent, wafting them in through open windows and doors.

We cannot see these arresting aromas in a picture; nevertheless, they epitomize the mood of the mediterranean garden more emphatically than much that is seen. Once experienced, these scents are never forgotten and will always have the power to conjure up that memory of a long summer afternoon in the mediterranean garden.

◀ The wooded hills shimmer blue-green through the warm afternoon haze, and the shade of an old linden tree *(Tilia X europaea)* dapples the forecourt of the farmhouse at Jas Crema near Carpentras in Haute Provence. This exquisite *provençal* garden was conceived and planted by the owner, Lulu de Waldner. Here, stone pavers are set in decomposed granite to make a firm, yet permeable, surface. Their colors, and that of the walls, blend so well, you must look twice to see they are not all one. An elegantly simple stone table invites you to sit and look over the rose-covered wall and down into the garden below.

◀ The late afternoon sun casts striking shadows against the warm pink wall of the house at Lotusland in Santa Barbara, California. A fanciful wrought-iron window grate, perfectly groomed golden barrel cactus *(Echinocactus grusonii)*, and volcanic stone mulch create a simple, but telling, dry-garden composition.

La Casella, near Grasse in southern France, is one of the most admired modern gardens of the Mediterranean region. The design of the main house was inspired by the pavilion for Mme. Pompadour at Fontainebleau, and the garden was designed by one of the owners, Claus Scheinert. The warm tomato-red house with dark blue shutters and door sets the French Mediterranean style. The whole scene is underscored by the dark shapes of Italian cypress *(Cupressus sempervirens)*, both sheared and natural. Paved with small round pebbles set on edge in a circular pattern, the forecourt centers around a tiled pool planted with water iris and edged with dwarf box *(Buxus sempervirens Suffruticosa)*. The round pool is accented by alternating pots of sheared bush germander *(Teucrium fruticans)* and wide buns of Japanese box *(Buxus microphylla japonica)*.

Decorated only by antique oil jars, this plain door to the private cultural foundation, Fundación Yannick y Ben Jakober, gives no hint of the spacious green interior patios beyond the walls. Isolated along the north coast of Majorca and surrounded by pine, the modern dwelling is designed like an enclosed fortified Arabian *ribat*, paying homage to Majorca's Moorish history.

▲ (Top) Even pottery celebrates the saturated colors and displays the flowers and fruits of the Mediterranean. Grapes and their viny tendrils weave among lemons, pomegranates, sunflowers, and a single pink *sempervirens* rose.

▲ (Above) A mediterranean garden is always about food and its distinctive flavors. Rosemary and lemon are two flavors that have enhanced many mediterranean dishes far back into history. Just the memory of Moroccan barbecued lamb, Greek lemon soup, or freshly baked Tuscan flatbread makes the mouth water in recognition.

◀ An imposing pergola, looking out over the valley, has been built on one terrace at La Casella. Its heavy beams and joists are supported by round brick columns made with *pianelle*, or curved bricks, in the Italian style. The permeable gravel paving lets every drop of winter rain penetrate to the roots. Behind, at the terrace wall, a visual rhythm is created by alternating forms of clipped greenery. Everything in the whole composition, save the potted ivy geranium, can live on winter rain alone, yet looks lush, green, and inviting.

▶ At Jas Crema, a wide garden arch in the French style is covered with the thornless banksia rose *(Rosa banksiae* 'Lutea'*)*. One of the best roses for a mediterranean climate, the Lady Banks rose blooms with clusters of small, bright yellow blossoms in early spring, after the wet winter. It then goes fairly dormant in the summer, tolerant of the dry soil and heat while remaining green. Mown grass paths in spring are let to go brown in summer, as this garden has no supplemental irrigation. The liberal planting of dark Italian cypress *(Cupressus sempervirens)* contrasts with the silvery foliage of the olive trees and highlights the garden's magnificent borrowed landscape, the medieval village of Le Barroux and its fortified keep.

A tough, old rambling rose, Phyllis Bide, climbs up the corner of this re-created French farmhouse in San Juan Capistrano, California. A vigorous grower, Phyllis Bide has almost no thorns and becomes quite tolerant of summer drought when older. The fragrant double blooms are borne in clusters and come continuously throughout the season. Their pinkish apricot color shows softly against the French limestone walls, and their scent envelops the bench below. Gravel paving and an old olive-oil jar complete the romantic mediterranean look.

◀ Below the rose-covered wall at Jas Crema, garden meets orchard in that sudden manner so typical of the mediterranean style. The old olive trees have been pollarded to promote the new growth that produces the best olives and makes the picking easier. Traditionally olive groves are underplanted with lavender to attract bees and increase the harvest; this plant association has become a signature of mediterranean garden design.

▲ The shaded terrace and walls of the gardener's cottage at La Casella are a plantsman's delight. White Japanese wisteria (Wisteria floribunda 'Longissima Alba') just dapples the gravel paving in May, then both foliage cover and shade become heavier with the warmth of summer. In the foreground, prostrate rosemary spills over the wall in front of pale yellow Sisyrinchium striatum. Behind, on the wall, a flannel bush (Fremontodendron californicum) splays out from the left, while a shrubby blue cape plumbago (Plumbago auriculata) reaches up into another vine for support.

◀ In the Southern California garden of Jacob and Gina Rabinovich, a broken-stone path under the arms of high, pruned olive trees invites you to the gated villa. Scented rosemary (*Rosmarinus officinalis* 'Tuscan Blue') and pink flowering rockrose (*Cistus X purpureus*) line the walk, with spires of Pride of Madeira (*Echium candicans*) looming behind. The walk is planted with *Dymondia margaretae* between the stones. Shrubs of bay laurel (*Laurus nobilis*) flank the covered gate, contributing to the mood of an Italian hillside.

▶ Terra-cotta stucco with milky blue shutters say *Provence*, while aromatic herbs flavor the air through the open casement. Rosemary drips over the old stone wall, and red valerian (*Centranthius ruber*) backs a mixed planting of green and gray lavender cotton (*Santolina chamaecyparissus* and *S. rosmarinifolia*) with white blooming germander (*Teucrium X lucidrys*).

◀ The garden at Clos du Peyronnet is carved into the rocky hillside above the Mediterranean Sea and the town of Menton-Garavan in France, close to the Italian border. Three generations of William Waterfield's family have lived and gardened there, each adding his or her own imprint on this gracious old garden. This vista is across two water lily ponds separated by a border of bearded iris, up a short flight of steps, and through an Italian style pergola, which is wreathed in a profusion of intertwined vines and capped by that old mediterranean favorite, the climbing rose La Follette.

▲ The Spanish influence on California's mediterranean style is clearly felt at the tiled entry of La
Casa Pacifica in San Clemente, California. Built in
the late 1920s as part of a large estate, it was
home to President Nixon and his wife during his
term of office. Privately owned today by Gavin and
Ninetta Herbert, the estate is gardened with great
taste and sensitivity to California's history and its
mediterranean climate. A soft buff-colored gravel
court sets off the dramatic forms of yucca *(Yucca
gloriosa)* and a New Zealand flax *(Phormium tenax)*.

▲ This Andalusian style courtyard with its high,
whitewashed walls is used as an outdoor room. It
is decorated with dozens of blooming begonias,
which are easy to water from a nearby water basin.
Under moving shade, both tuberous and cane-type
begonias flourish alongside the ubiquitous impatiens *(Impatiens walleriana)*. These tender, succulent
perennials give color throughout summer and will
only droop when they need water.

▶ A beautifully planted walk steps down to a cupola, which looks out over the Mediterranean Sea at Marimurta Botanical Garden in Calella de Palafrugell, Spain. The alternating forms of citrus and cypress set a visual rhythm that is punctuated by the cascading forms of rosea ice plant (*Drosanthemum floribundum*) at each level. Located along the rugged Costa Brava, where the Pyrenees plunge to the sea, this inspiring garden has no irrigation system and depends entirely on winter rains.

▼ From within the shade of a small pavilion, one can peer through the foliage of bougainvillea to a unique clipped garden at Villa Noailles near Grasse, France. Made entirely with santolina—gray *Santolina chamaecyparissus* and green *S. rosmarinifolia*—punctuated by balls of box *(Buxus sempervirens)*, the narrow space is visually elongated by the design. Although made as recently as the 1960s, this garden recalls the Viscount Charles de Noailles's interest in cubism.

▶ Imagine dining at this table, where the wine is cooled in the center water trough, and the guests are cooled by running water at their feet. The magnificent stone table stands at the center of the famous garden at Villa Lante in Bagnia, Italy. Considered the greatest surviving Renaissance garden, Villa Lante takes the form of several shallow terraces rising up the hillside behind the Fountain of the Giant River Gods. This symmetrical garden is almost a mirror image of itself on each side, divided down its central axis by different displays of water. It demonstrates a perfect balance between sun and shade, clipped greenery and stone.

▲ A lone olive tree softens the grand celebration of mediterranean colors at the Matisse Museum, above Nice in southern France. The faux shuttered windows look down on a simple court of decomposed granite.

◀ The house at Le Domaine du Vignole is a rescued and restored *bastide* farm-manor house from the sixteenth century. The modern garden, designed by famous French landscape architect Jean Mus, reflects the property's agricultural heritage while adhering to the naturalistic planting style of today. The broad swaths of green and gray santolina *(Santolina chamaecyparissus* and *S. ros-marinifolia)* in front of the closely shorn dark forms of Italian cypress *(Cupressus sempervirens)* and yew *(Taxus baccata)* create a powerful rhythm of sculptural forms against the vine-covered house. Informal drifts of subtle color and contrasting texture, punctuated with massive dark exclamation points, are the backbone of this elegant garden's design.

Generous steps of decomposed granite, retained with railroad ties, lead to the covered porch of this gracious old farmhouse called La Pomme d'Ambre, near the ancient port town of Fréjus in southern France. The master gardener here is the owner, a plant collector and naturalist. Her passion for native Mediterranean plants is as strong as her eye for design, so her garden speaks to every kind of gardener. The terraces and terra-cotta pots that line the steps are overflowing with unrecognizable species and cultivars, each well grown, trained, and displayed to its best advantage.

The house at La Casella in southern France sits on one of a series of broad, shallow terraces, which then stretch out to the west. These were once olive terraces laboriously leveled and retained with beautiful dry-stone walls. Some of the old olive trees have been kept and rejuvenated by careful pruning; their picturesque gnarled trunks lend a feeling of age to the sixteen-year-old garden. Look closely to see the engrossing tension created by delicate balance: of age and youth, of hard architectural forms and greenery, of tightly clipped forms and abundant flowing ones.

▼ This rough-hewn Majorcan garden gate swings against a sandstone rock. The sun shines hot, so the shade within beckons, but the aloe *(Aloe lutescens)* blooms undaunted.

◄ Villa le Balze is tucked into the side of one of the hills of Fiesole. Built in 1912 by the British architects Cecil Pinsent and Geoffrey Scott, it completely recaptures the precepts of Italian Renaissance design. The villa's powerful simplicity never detracts from the magnificent view, and its landscaping exhibits a harmonious pairing of clipped greenery and classical stonework.

The practice of pollarding plane trees *(Platanus acerifolia)* each winter creates a spot of low, leafy shade during the summer. This pruning practice not only keeps large-growing trees lower, it also encourages the production of larger individual leaves. At Château Brantes in Sorgues, France, summer dining by the reflecting pool is a cool delight because of this living canopy. The deciduous plane trees are bare during winter when the warmth of the sun is welcomed. Another cooling device found in mediterranean climates is that of growing Boston ivy *(Parthenocissus tricuspidata)* or Virginia creeper *(P. quinquefolia)* on south and west walls. These deciduous clinging vines cool the house in the summer and let in the warming winter sun. Both vines must be kept under control by annual winter pruning.

ENDLESS SUNSHINE— PRECIOUS WATER

Sunshine is the most defining element of a mediterranean garden. Even though the warmth of the morning sun is welcome, the heat of midday and afternoon demands shady relief. Ideas for using sun and creating shade have been found in garden drawings and writings from ancient Persia, Egypt, and the Roman Empire. The great chronicler Pliny the Younger (A.D. 61–113) wrote of a detached room of cool marble in his own garden. It was open on all sides but covered with vines, which hung down to the ground. He liked to rest there in the airy green shade and remember what it was like to lie in the woods.

Arbors and pergolas—covered with roses, gourds, and other types of vines— are pictured in Roman frescoes dating from the fourth century A.D. These structures look much the same as those built in mediterranean gardens today. In both, shady enclosures and long pergolas alternate with open vistas. Thus, as we stroll through the garden, we pass through a cool, shaded space into a wide, sun-drenched view of the sea, the countryside, or the rest of the garden. In a bright, arid climate, this dramatic contrast provides a breathtaking experience.

Centuries of trial and error have proved some trees to be favorites for shade-making. Most popular are broad-leafed, deciduous trees such as the mulberry, linden, horse chestnut, and plane tree—usually pollarded to encourage low branching and large leaves. Their leafy cover lends cooling shade in summer, and then goes bare in winter to let in the warming sun.

Evergreen trees are important as well, and traditional examples such as olives, oaks, bay laurel, and sometimes pepper trees *(Schinus molle)* are still popular shade-makers. Modern gardens are being made today in Mediterranean areas that once were terraced olive groves. Old, beautifully gnarled olive trees are saved and incorporated as the backbone of what is, essentially, a new garden. In California, field-grown olive trees are trucked in and planted to impart that same feeling of maturity.

Evergreen oaks are always valued for their cool, dense shade. Some California gardens have inherited one or more types of native oak: coast live oak *(Quercus agrifolia)*, canyon live oak *(Q. chrysolepis)*, or Engelmann oak *(Q. engelmannii)*. With careful avoidance of any change to their environment, these majestic creatures will outlive several human generations.

The Mediterranean Holm oak *(Quercus ilex)* is appreciated in California gardens as well as in its native haunts. Tough and adaptable, it can be trained and shaped to fit any garden size and need, from screening hedge to spreading tree. Garden use of this tree goes back a long way. Italian Renaissance gardens usually had a planted oak woodland nearby, called the *selvatico* or *bosco*. It offered the same cool respite from the sun that Pliny spoke of so fondly centuries earlier.

Planting oaks and other trees in a grid pattern seems to be a new garden-design trend in California. Actually this pat-terning dates back to early Moorish orchard gardens where trees were geometrically spaced along irrigation channels—another example of necessity fostering a garden-design tradition.

Precious water is the other defining element of the mediterranean garden. In the earliest Persian gardens it was the symbol of purity and life. The Islamic garden was designed to represent the Garden of Paradise. At its very center was a calm circle of water, which appeared to emerge from the earth. It allowed one to gaze at the reflection of sky and stars, and by seeing the connection between heaven and earth, one could find the spiritual connection between life here and in the hereafter. A perfectly quiet pool brings the sky down into the modern garden as well. Although its ancient meaning may no longer be well known, one can still feel awe and reverence by gazing down into the stillness.

Even before its symbolic occurrence in the early Islamic garden, water was regarded as sacred. Genesis recounts: "A river went out of Eden to water the garden; and from thence it was parted and became four heads." These spilled out in four directions and represented the four rivers of Paradise, dividing the world into four sections. In the garden, emerging from the central pool or "spring of life," these "rivers"

The dark mouth of a cool grotto entices you to explore its interior, just as it must have done for garden visitors in the sixteenth century, when the magnificent Villa Lante was built. Cut into the retaining wall at the side of the Fountain of Lights, the grotto is dedicated to Venus, the Roman goddess of gardens who was born of the sea; its twin on the other side is dedicated to Neptune, the Roman god of the sea and water. These watery gods symbolized the attributes of the garden to the classically educated Renaissance man.

An authentic fourteenth-century grotto from the Italian Renaissance
is found at the end of the pergola in the garden of the Villa Massai
owned by Gil Cohen and Paul Gervais, author of the book *A Garden
in Lucca*. One is drawn into the cool, dark interior of the grotto by
the sound of trickling water, which flows from the mouth of a mask
into a basin below. The area abounds with natural springs, and it is
likely this grotto was built on the site of an earlier Roman one.

were represented by water runnels that divided the garden into the symbolic *chahar bagh* or four-part design, still seen in many mediterranean gardens today. Then as well as now, this precise man-made geometry was softened by planting.

Centuries later, the Romans recognized the importance of water for the well-being of their gardens. They built aqueducts to bring water down from the mountains, and cisterns in which to store it for later use. Even the most modest dwelling excavated at Pompeii had a small pool or fountain in the peristyle garden both to cool the air and irrigate the plants. The gravity-fed fountain ran only on special occasions, requiring a servant to climb up on the roof and fill the water tank.

During the Italian Renaissance, water became an important symbol of conspicuous consumption. This was a period of vast villa building, and the lavish display of water became yet one more demonstration of wealth and power. Huge fountains thundered and roared; smaller, more intricate ones sprayed and spewed; water jets animated moving sculpture and squirted unsuspecting guests. Long before electricity, the hydraulics engineer was as important to gardens as the architect.

Centuries later, during the Victorian era, history repeated itself. This was a time when the elite of Europe flocked to the Riviera and built extravagant estates for the winter social season. So, once again, outrageous and excessive displays of precious water in this dry climate became symbols of affluence and influence.

At least a thousand years ago, the Arabic garden makers of Morocco and southern Spain, already masters of hydrology and irrigation, invented a water-lifting device called the *Persian Wheel*. With it they brought water up from wells and diverted it from natural springs and rivers into canals, which

Grotesque masks dribble water on the side walls of the grotto at Villa Massai. These fierce faces often guarded ancient Roman grottoes, which were thought to represent openings to the underworld.

fed into long, narrow irrigation channels modeled after those of ancient Egypt. This laboriously built system provided precious water to their orchards and crop gardens, which were laid out in a formal grid pattern.

Later, as these channels were decoratively lined and tiled, they became an integral part of the garden design. Richly ornamented, some channels were widened into rectangular pools, while others ran from courtyard to courtyard. Enclosed orchard gardens featured an irrigation-based grid layout for both fruit and ornamental plants. Thus, a design tradition was born, displaying an economy of water usage that is as relevant today as it was then.

These are historical precedents for the ways we use water and shade in modern sun-drenched gardens. This sense of refreshment, which cannot be seen, is far more important to a mediterranean garden than colorful flower borders. The elements of water and shade will always be the most important sources of sensory delight in the warm, dry mediterranean climate.

◀ A perfectly round water-lily pool is the focus of one garden room at La Casella. Not only water lilies, but also water iris, water hyacinth, and common calla lilies *(Zantedeschia aethiopica)* flourish among the koi fish. Fishing line is strung across the pond to protect the fish from nighttime predators. The pool is edged with young citrus trees planted in the ground, in potted standards, and in cones. A clipped hedge of arborvitae *(Thuja orientalis)* forms the background and separates this garden room from the one on the terrace below.

▲ The display of running water is fittingly modest in modern mediterranean style gardens. At La Casella a placid-looking sphinx barely dribbles into the shell basin below. This is enough, however, to create a cooling sensation along the garden walk. You need only hear the sound of water in a garden to feel soothed and refreshed.

◀ From inside a cool, dark loggia, one looks out into the young mediterranean style garden of Jacob and Gina Rabinovich in Southern California. In the foreground, the traditional quadripartite design with a central pool is outlined in box hedges. Field-grown olive trees are pruned to cast shadows against pale ocher-pink walls, which are beginning to be draped with prostrate rosemary. These elements, along with the sound of the trickling fountain, all contribute to a sun-drenched mood.

▼ Although no shade is cast, the classic rose arches at Jas Crema form a visual bower of color. Underplanted with lavender, the small climbing rose, Tea Rambler, provides summer fragrance and pale pink embroidery to the edge of the garden. This garden, done by its owner Lulu de Waldner, captures both the French love of design and the English love of flowers.

▶ Based on the idea of a French *tèse*, a path through a shady tunnel of green clipped shrubs, these arches function as doorways to sequential rooms in a modern mediterranean style garden. Tough and dry-soil tolerant, purple hop bush *(Dodonaea viscosa* 'Purpurea'*)* in the foreground and Victorian box *(Pittosporum undulatum)* in the background are good, large shrubs for this use.

◀ The exquisite twin pavilions at Villa Lante in Bagnia, Italy, are set like marble jewels at the highest elevation of the garden. They enclose the Fountain of the Deluge, which is the water source for the whole garden. The severe Roman-inspired Renaissance architecture is augmented by crayfish medallions. This stated to all who could read the iconography that its sixteenth-century owner, Cardinal Gambera (which means crayfish), was an educated classicist and humanist scholar. Much simpler pavilions are found in today's gardens, where they carry on the tradition of offering a cool retreat from the hot sun.

◄ Renaissance garden-makers were masters of creating sensory delight. The lower terrace of the Villa Medici is backed by a high retaining wall. Along its base runs an elevated walk covered by a long pergola, which invites you to stroll under the dappled shade of climbing roses and gaze out at the panoramic view over Florence and the Arno valley. The plantings are plain and simple, designed to complement the breathtaking view rather than to compete with it. By the time you reach the sun-filled end of the pergola, you are cooled and refreshed by shade and the uphill breeze.

◄ A Tuscan style pergola has round columns built with curved bricks called *pianelle*. These have been made in Italy since the time of the Romans, when the columns were plastered to resemble stone. The use of unmilled wood for beams and joists, supporting the rose across the top, is also typical. These elements, plus the planting of irises along the path, create an air of traditional rustic simplicity.

▶ Mediterranean colors warm this modernist interpretation of the classic Spanish patio. Famed Spanish landscape architect Fernando Caruncho employed minimalist geometry for this Majorcan house. Enclosed on three sides, the patio concentrates the scents of wisteria and jasmine. The vines will soon lap the top of the metal arbor and provide shade for the patio and arcade. Potted boxwood *(Buxus sempervirens)* relieves the expanse of concrete steps.

▼ A traditional shading device in a mediterranean garden is the vine-covered trellis. The house at Clos du Peyronnet in Menton, France, has a south-facing terrace, its trellis wreathed with an ancient wisteria. The woody deciduous vine has been used for this purpose for hundreds of years. Because it is bare in winter and thick with cool shade in summer, the wisteria offers ideal climate control.

▼ A wrought-iron eyebrow trellis caps the doors and windows of this thick-walled French *provençal* style house. The graceful supports hold three flat iron rods, just enough to display the grapevine and its eventual fruit against the ocher-yellow walls.

▲ The *boschetto* at the very end of the long, narrow garden at Villa le Balze is a twentieth-century reinter-pretation of the classic Italian Renaissance *bosco*. Created by English architects Geoffrey Scott and Cecil Pinsent, the villa stands as an exquisite example of the Renaissance style. The evergreen, native holly oaks *(Quercus ilex)* have served as shade trees all around the Mediterranean for hundreds of years. Tough, adapt-able, and amenable to pruning, these beautiful trees can be grown in any mediterranean climate.

▶ A magnificent date palm *(Phoenix dactylifera)* casts a dramatic shadow across the doorway at El Laberinto d'Horta in Barcelona, Spain. These towering palms have been grown along the Mediterranean Sea for at least five thousand years, producing one of the earliest commercial crops known to man.

▲ The pollarded *Platanus X acerifolia*, or plane trees as they are called in Europe, begin in May to form their shady summer arcade over the drive from the gate to the house at Le Vignole. Designed by French landscape architect Jean Mus, who is known for his creative use of indigenous Mediterranean plants, the garden needs little, if any, supplemental irrigation.

◄ A soft, silvery gray palette predominates in the mediterranean style garden. Many plants originating in this climate have adapted to the intense summer sunlight by developing leaves that reflect light and protect them from dehydration. Their hairy or glaucous gray-green surfaces read silver or gray to the eye and produce a soft look. The Olive Garden at La Landriana in Tor San Lorenzo, Italy, displays this kind of softness. Even in early summer, without flower color, this garden beckons you down its shadow-strewn path with a gentle gray invitation.

▶ The Fountain of Lights at Villa Lante was originally called the Water Organ because it could once be played upon as if it were a musical instrument. Created in 1564 by Thomas Chiruchi, a Siennese hydraulics specialist, together with the artist Giacomo da Vignola, it was one of the first water automata. These popular Renaissance garden features were usually animal sculptures animated by water power and accompanied by acoustic effects.

◀ The water parterre at Villa Gamberaia may be the most famous water-oriented garden feature in Italy, even though it boasts no great splashing. The classically proportioned garden with four shallow rectangular reflecting pools, a central round gold-fish pond, and a terminal semicircular lily pool has been called a horizontal hall of mirrors. It certainly feels that way as you wander through, watching the duplicating reflections of perfectly shaped, simple topiary. These include box, yew, and a breathtaking giant ball of *Phillyria latifolia*. Here and there, in small corners or pots, colorful annuals and pelargoniums are used with great restraint, and only as accents. The whole is enclosed with clipped Italian cypress, which takes the form of a theatrical *palissade* at the end. This encloses the garden while drawing you to the sweeping view of the valley below.

◀ A shady gallery of clipped bay laurel *(Laurus nobilis)* runs the length of the Villa Aurelia garden at the American Academy in Rome. A walk through its scented green darkness cools and refreshes the spirit, so important on a hot summer day. Sweet bay, as it is sometimes called, is a Mediterranean native, the use of which goes back to ancient history, when Delphic priestesses induced their prophecies by breathing the smoke of bay leaves. Crowns for victors and heroes have always been made of bay laurel, giving rise to the term *baccalaureate*.

◀ Pools and fountains in the shape of an eight-pointed star are commonly found in gardens in Spain and California. This geometric form is an inheritance of Islamic culture, brought by the Moors when they ruled the Spanish peninsula. The eight-pointed star is actually a square within a square, a shape of deep religious significance to the faith. Filling this form with precious and purifying water is thought to reinforce the symbolic relationship between heaven and earth. One can somehow feel this ancient message by observing the sky reflected in the pool and rill behind the main house at Lotusland in Santa Barbara, California.

▶ The tiled catch basin at the end of the rill is a circle within a square, complete with its own tiny fountain.

▶ The famous musical water cascade at Villa Lante not only divides the garden laterally, it forms the garden's very backbone. Called *cantena d'aqua* (water chain), the falling water literally makes its own music as it swirls its way down the gentle slope. A masterpiece of stone and water sculpture by the Italian Renaissance artist and architect Giacomo da Vignola, it is designed in the form of an elongated crayfish to signify the name of the garden's owner, Cardinal Gambera.

This traditional Spanish style fountain with multiple thin jets arching into a rectangular pool is modeled after the famous canal-like example in the Patio de la Acequia of the Generalife in Granada. The rectangular pool design is based on early Moorish irrigation canals, and the spouting circular fountain in the foreground has its roots in the central round pool of the Islamic Paradise garden. This re-creation is in the heart of a public garden in Palma, Majorca.

A Hispano-Moorish rectangular pool with thin spouting jets forms the central axis in the modern Santa Barbara garden of Mr. and Mrs. Malcolm McDuffie. Landscape architect Sydney Baumgartner has created a mediterranean style garden using elements from several traditions. The allée of non-fruiting olive trees *(Olea europaea* 'Skylark Dwarf'*)* in large terra-cotta pots is underplanted with lavender *(Lavandula intermedia)*. The grid of young plane trees *(Platinus X acerifolia)* will soon cast summer shade for the seating area on the terrace, while the small fountain cools the air and makes soft garden music. Another mediterranean touch is the Boston Ivy *(Parthenocissis tricuspidata)*, which clothes the chimney around the old Portuguese tile composite.

◀ In the central fountain of the Fern Garden at Casa del Herrero in Santa Barbara, California, water spills out into a tiled pool copied from Hispano-Moorish gardens. This is the most meaningful shape of all in Islamic art: a circle within a square, heaven brought to earth and earth reflecting heaven, within a perfect and sacred geometric form.

▲ A modern entry courtyard in California is graced with the sound of water. The round cement pool features two recirculating wall fountains, back to back. The yellow flag (*Iris pseudacorus*) and water lilies (*Nymphaea* species) thrive in the shallow pond along with a few goldfish, which control the mosquito larvae. The circular paved area is bordered by Japanese boxwood (*Buxus japonica*), and the stones are interplanted with *Dymondia margaretae*.

▲ In southern France, water features in gardens are often old, reclaimed town wellheads, or copies of them. On the terrace at Jas Crema, water dribbles from a re-created spigot into the simple stone trough below.

◀ The spectacular eight-pointed star fountain in the rear garden at Casa del Herrero is the centerpiece of the narrowing allée that runs the length of the garden. Built in the early 1900s by early Santa Barbara landscape architect Ralph Stevens in collaboration with the owners, Mr. and Mrs. George Fox Steedman, the garden is a superb example of the influence of Spanish architecture and design on California estates of that time. The Moorish pools, rill, and fountains visually connect the series of descending, narrowing patios and elongate the perspective.

▲ You can almost hear the quiet splash of water running off the stepped, tiled rill and into this catch basin with its pierced openings. These tiles and those found throughout the garden at Casa del Herrero are copies of Spanish tile.

▼ Splashing water from two fountains, each with its tiny
rill flowing into the fishpond, cools the air in this Spanish
garden. The connecting patios are located in the center of
the Moorish *ribat*-inspired house, and the soothing sound
of water can be heard from every room. Box-lined beds
are thickly planted with fruit and ornamentals, relieving
the traditional white walls with their color and texture.
The tiled arcade opens to views down the northern coast
of Majorca to the Mediterranean Sea beyond.

▶ Even a swimming pool can contribute to the sound of
water in the garden. The McElwee garden in Capistrano
Beach, California, has an old well-head that dribbles
recirculated water into the pool. Flanked by two potted
'Nagami' kumquats, with a living mulch of Australian violet
(*Viola hederacea*), the reclaimed statue of Saint Fiacre is the
focal point of the rear patio. A dark hedge of purple hop bush
(*Dodonaea viscosa* 'Purpurea') behind the graveled terrace
silhouettes the statue, and a huge old Aleppo pine (*Pinus
halepensis*) and a Canary Island palm (*Phoenix canariensis*)
tower beyond. Dark, clipped buns of potted juniper
(*Juniperus chinensis* 'Blue Point') and Japanese box (*Buxus
japonica* 'Green Beauty') complete the mediterranean picture.

◀ Densely obscured by shrubbery, the five descending pools at Clos du Peyronnet nevertheless link the top of the terraced garden with the Mediterranean Sea in the distance. Each pool is located on a different terrace and spills quietly to the one below, thus forming a powerful visual axis and connection to the sea.

◀ When all else fails and there is no water available, plant a water feature like this one at the Jardin Exotique in Monaco. Using the foliage of blue ice plant *(Senecio mandraliscae)* to represent water, and the round forms of barrel cactus *(Echinocactus)* to represent boulders and tumbled rocks, the designer has created the feeling of a creek running with water.

LIVING
OUTDOORS

An inviting daybed on the shaded porch of this French farmhouse entices you to sit, lie back, and put your feet up, surrounded by the sights and sounds of the garden. A rose and a jasmine are planted nearby to float their scent in through the open doors. The pillows, tablecloth, and drape all echo the motifs and colors of the *provençal* garden, where outdoor living is celebrated.

We live in an age when more and more human activity takes place indoors: inside rooms, inside air-conditioned buildings and vehicles, inside cubicles. But humankind has always had a need to be in the open air, close to nature, near other living species. Think how much of our best art and music represent this human desire to be outdoors.

Perhaps our common need to be outside can explain the increasing popularity of gardening in modern society. However, even Pliny, the first-century Roman, wanted a place in his garden to dream of lying in the woods. And where better to satisfy this longing for nature than in one's own garden, especially when it has been created as a space of sanctuary? Enclosed and protected by vines, shrubs, and trees from the stress of modern living, yet open to the sky, the breeze, and the sound of birds and insects, the garden nourishes the human soul.

Today, many people want to live in a mediterranean climate. The winters are relatively mild, the springs are gloriously colorful, and the long summer heat is dry. It is this dry air that discourages insects, making it pleasant to live outdoors—to work and play, to cook, to spread a table and dine, to relax, even to make a bed and sleep. Mediterranean gardens have always been planned with these outdoor pleasures in mind.

Archeologists have discovered that early Romans designed their houses with a central or rear atrium. This was a room open to both the sky and the dwelling. It was separated from the living areas only by a covered peristyle, shielded from the weather by curtains. Simple plantings of herbs and a small gravity-fed water fountain refreshed the air in the atrium garden. Even before the Romans, the ancient Egyptians used open porticoes to bring the outdoor air into their living spaces. Italian Renaissance architects built on this idea, designing residences such as Villa Gamberaia with an interior courtyard and Villa Medici with an open loggia. In southern Spain, the architectural model of an enclosed patio open to the sky is widespread, and can be traced back long before the Moors arrived, to the Roman occupation. Modern architects and designers bring the outdoors in by opening up the walls of a house in a variety of ways, re-creating the ancient Roman notion of indoor/outdoor living.

Highly ornamented grottoes became fashionable during the Renaissance, and no garden was complete without its re-creation of a cave decorated in mosaic, with bits of marble, *spugna*, coal, and shells. Ancient caves, especially those with natural springs, were venerated places. The early Greeks relied completely on water from springs, and these natural features were so important to life that they became endowed with spiritual meaning. Dedicated to the particular

nymph who lived there, the natural grotto became a religious shrine, adorned with statuary and flowers. Romans, with their superior plumbing technology, carried this a step further. They built architectural grottoes where piped-in water spilled from a statue or from the open mouth of a mask. Called *nymphaea*, these grottoes were embellished with mosaic tiles or finished on the inner surfaces with pumice to give the rustic look of a natural grotto. The grotto became part of the Roman garden, easily accessible for offerings to the particular god or goddess to whom it was dedicated.

Sixteen centuries later, Italian Renaissance designers drew their inspiration from ancient Greece and Rome, and the grotto reappeared as a garden feature. Ornamented with designs of colored stone, fitted with its statue of a Roman deity, often spouting water, the Renaissance grotto retained the ancient pagan vocabulary but was stripped of its religious importance. As visitors walked through the garden, the grotto was a welcome retreat to bathe hands and face, to rest, and to escape the heat of the day.

Walls are as important to a garden as they are to a house. They serve to surround and protect, to define outdoor rooms, and to establish privacy. In small gardens, walls create a feeling of more space by blocking views of the entire garden at one

The idea of an open interior courtyard dates back to Roman times. The American Academy in Rome, built in 1912 to designs by McKim, Mead and White, honors that ancient tradition. Centered around three old Italian cypress *(Cupressus sempervirens)* and a fountain by sculptor Paul Manship, the courtyard opens off the arcaded piano nobile. Scented star jasmine *(Trachelospermum jasminoides)*, which clothes the columns, and the splashing water both refresh the atmosphere. The floor is paved with pebbles and marble chips, carefully chosen to complement the warm colors of the building.

Nestled by a wall, protected from the cold mistral, is the perfect outdoor nook for a morning latté. An old tree branch and Virginia creeper (Parthenocissus quinquefolia) create a living piece of art against the apricot-colored stones. And, although gardeners seldom sit, it is pleasant to have a spot such this where one can stop and reflect on the garden.

glance. Although walls are not unique to mediterranean gardens, they are common in this climate, with all its outdoor activity. Within a garden, walls need not be solid or high. They may be as thin as a fence or a lattice strung with vines, or may take the form of espaliered fruit or flowering trees.

See-through or windowed, rows of sheared evergreen shrubs in the form of hedges are an effective way to create walls and define areas. Depending on the plants used, they can rise to a towering wall overhead, or hunker all the way down to a tiny six-inch edging. Hedges need not be squared off either; they can be sheared into rounded and undulating forms to create an illusion of movement in the garden. Two or more species of shrubs with similar growth habits but different colored leaves are sometimes planted together along a hedgerow. As they intertwine, with repeated shearings a tapestry-like effect is created on the face of the hedge. This is often done with all green and variegated varieties of the same plant, such as Italian buckthorn *(Rhamnus alaternus)* or the purple-leaved and green-leaved selections of hop bush *(Dodonaea viscosa)*. It is most effective on taller hedges where the patterning can be easily seen.

People continue to find new ways to live outdoors and extend the time spent there. In a mediterranean climate, indoor/outdoor activity goes on almost all year round, and those who live in these places enjoy a close awareness of nature, and of the seasons. Even with today's air conditioning, we like to gather with friends around outdoor fireplaces and dining tables, to enjoy the food cooked on outdoor barbecues. Outdoor beds in the form of hammocks, chaises longues, and day beds offer a place to nap and "dream of lying in the woods." Adventurous souls install outdoor showers and bathtubs. Just imagine the luxuriousness of a bath among the bulrushes!

▼ The rear terrace of Wally and Susie Moore's reconstructed French farmhouse in Southern California is a good place to lunch and relax in the shade. The stone pavers are interplanted with different cultivars of thyme. Roses pop out of every planting space and are deftly trained up the walls as well.

▲ The walled herb garden at Jas Crema, in the Valucluse region of France, exemplifies the exquisite planning and detailing its creator, Lulu de Waldner, is known for. There are nine identical rectangular beds, each featuring an Italian cypress growing in a sunken pot to limit its size. Some beds are devoted to culinary herbs, such as chives, sage, tarragon, and mint. Others are filled with blooming ornamentals. A row of large pots along the porch holds identical plants of rare rosebud-flowered pelargonium. Wisteria is being trained flat up against the tall outer wall. Beyond, the garden gives way to an olive orchard, a natural transition into the countryside.

▶ Viscount Charles de Noailles developed his garden above Grasse in the late 1940s. On a steep hillside previously terraced with olive trees, the garden has been known from its beginning as a plantsman's paradise. English in style, but planted with many mediterranean as well as temperate-climate species, Villa Noailles straddles two traditions. Circular stone steps descend from one terrace that is bordered with winter-flowering shrubs and an "English lawn" in the center. On each side, the viscount built matching small pavilions with pointed roofs as a tribute to his friend Lawrence Johnston and the garden at Hidcote.

◀ A lacy pattern of shade from a locust tree *(Robinia X ambigua 'Decaisneana')* decorates the gravel terrace at the Pasadena home of Bruce and Regina Drucker. This tough and drought-tolerant tree is a wise choice for a graveled area, where its shallow suckering roots can be monitored. An espaliered loquat *(Eriobotrya deflexa)* spans the wall behind, and the house walls are insulated with Boston ivy *(Parthenocissus tricuspidata.)* Combined with the terra-cotta pot, these elements express a mediterranean style for the outdoor dining area.

▲ The forecourt at Jas Crema is dominated by three old trees—two plane trees *(Platanus X acerifolia)* and a linden *(Tilia X europaea).* Their high shade cools the outdoor living areas. Dry-laid stone paving wraps around a small patch of lawn—just enough for visiting children to play upon. A row of Italian cypress relieves the plain face of the *bastide* farmhouse, and Virginia creeper *(Parthenocissus quinquefolia)* is beginning to creep across the ocher-pink walls.

▶ At Villa di Geggiano, near Sienna, Italy, the sixteenth-century foyer extends right through the center of the house, indicating that it may once have been a carriageway through the *piano terreno,* with the *piano nobile* a floor above. During the eighteenth century, the passage was covered with these soft renditions of bucolic scenes, done by an itinerant painter, so that the family could enjoy scenes of eternal spring in the countryside every day of the year.

▼ One of the twin pavilions at the highest terrace of the garden at Villa Lante still retains some of its original frescoes. Its pillared open wall catches the breeze and overlooks the garden below. The interiors were originally completely covered with murals dedicated to the Greek muses. These were the nine daughters of Zeus who inspired and presided over the creative arts. One holds a stringed instrument and is probably Polyhymnia, the muse of sacred song.

▶ The famed British architect Cecil Pinsent designed this re-creation of a Renaissance grotto at Villa le Balze in the early twentieth century. Cut into the steep rocks of Fiesole above Florence, the grotto is decorated with busts of Aristotle, Socrates, Demosthenes, and Zeno in honor of the owner, American philosopher and scholar Charles Augustus Strong. It is called the Triton Grotto, after the mythical sea god who rides a dolphin and dribbles cool water into the pool below. Presiding over all, in her own *spugna*-encrusted niche, stands Venus. To the ancients, Venus was not only the goddess of love, beauty, and the garden, but was, like Triton, born of the sea, so statues honoring her were often placed in grottoes to reinforce their watery meaning.

▲ One of the delights at Villa Gamberaia, northeast of Florence, is this narrow garden sliced out of the terracing on either side. Called the *cabinet di roccaglia,* or richly encrusted small room, its curving walls are covered in ancient *pietra dura,* from which most of the colored marble tesserae have long since disappeared. Niches with terra-cotta peasant figures and a lovely sandstone fountain in the shape of a wide urn define the curving space. Pink hydrangeas grow in traditional Italian terra-cotta pots, and an ancient wisteria wreathes the stairs. The steps were fitted with water jets operated from below in order to startle garden visitors. Called *giocci d'acqua,* these "wet surprises" were the fashion in Baroque gardens.

◀ A close-up view shows the *pietra dura* technique used to decorate walls, niches, and grottoes. A Roman river god with his cornucopia reclines on a rocky couch. Fashioned of carved limestone and colored stones and decorated with chips of marble, coal, and a limestone deposit called *spugna*, he brings richness and plenty to the garden. Notice the edging of tiny cockleshells, which historically were used to reinforce the connection to Venus, as in the famous Botticelli painting.

▲ The original designers of Villa Gamberaia have not been documented, only the series of owners. Records and inscriptions date the original layout to 1610, so it is a true creation of the Renaissance. This mysterious garden feature most certainly dates from that time. Called the *Nymphaeum*, which was the Latin name given to the first man-made grottoes, it is the destination at the very end of a long grass allée. Within a large niche encrusted with *spugna* looms the figure thought to be Pan or Dionysus. He has horns, he brandishes a trident, lions guard his side, and what is left of an eagle perches on his shoulder. Water trickles from the top of a mossy rock into a pool.

▶ At each end of the Orange Garden at Villa le Balze, architect Cecil Pinsent placed an ornamental niche enclosing an urn, richly decorated with *pietra dura*. This early-twentieth-century outdoor room in the Italian style would have been incomplete without enclosing walls and these Renaissance embellishments. The flanking pink oleanders *(Nerium oleander)* are basic shrubs throughout Italy and the rest of the Mediterranean, but there is an old country warning about this poisonous plant: "He who sleeps under an oleander never wakes up!"

◀ A lovely chipped-stone table and a pair of rustic chairs make an outdoor dining room on this terrace in the California garden of designer Julie Heinsheimer. Cut stone squares in the rosy-toned gravel provide a firm surface for chair legs, and the deciduous fruit trees overhead shade the terrace in summer. Rosemary billows out over the retaining wall and scents the air. Bearded irises are just about ready to decorate the scene with their jewel-like colors.

▶ Wide French doors open onto the shaded grassy terrace of this inspiring little garden in the tiny village of Cabriz, France. This is the haunt of a real gardener whose passion for roses is combined with a love of the history of this area, now known as "Riviera backcountry." Wanting her garden to reflect that heritage, she called on her friend, landscape architect Jean Mus, for the design. He carved out a garden from the steep terraced hillside around the new house, leaving in place the best of the old olive trees and high-lighting the original rock retaining walls. Native shrubs, such as lentisc (*Pistacia lentiscus*) and cistus species mingle together with shrub roses to belly out over the walls, and a wine grape clambers up and over the wrought-iron eyebrow trellis.

▲ Enclosing walls are important protection from the drying mistral winds in southern France, between Aix and the Luberon. They also make possible this flawless little garden by the edge of the terrace at Château Val Joanis. A tousle of gray and green foliage with pink and apricot blooms foams over the edge and up the soft honey-colored wall. The meticulously clipped cones of yew and the charming little wire chairs contribute to the *provençal* look.

This clipped green palisade defines one edge of the Spanish Patio at Casa del Herrero in Santa Barbara, California. Completely covered with creeping fig (Ficus pumula), the original stucco arcade looks like living green architecture. Noted architect George Washington Smith designed the house for Mr. and Mrs. George Fox Steedman in the early 1900s. Although he designed in several Mediterranean styles, he was most known for Spanish Colonial in the Andalusian mode, with its off-center, irregular window placements. Typically Moorish, the patio was copied from one in the Alhambra, and has a small water fountain on the wall at one end.

This magnificent maze of cypress hedges was part of an estate built in 1799 by the Marquises of Alfarràs, outside of Barcelona. Labyrinths were a popular garden feature in the eighteenth century, and El Laberinto d'Horta is one of the few remaining examples of that forgotten art. From the top of the terrace, one can see the pond and several statues of mythological figures within the hedging. There is a marble plaque at the entry showing Ariadne giving Theseus the thread that will permit him to find his way back out of the fabled maze of ancient Crete.

A chipped-stone table on the gravel terrace at Château Brantes offers a place to display garden ornament. The pollarded mulberry trees *(Morus species)* will soon fill in with their summer growth, shading the terrace for dining and conversation. Planting trees directly in gravel or decomposed granite paving is a sensible tradition in mediterranean gardens. Rain can penetrate directly through the surface to the roots, and there is no need for the unsightly edging used to protect trees planted in lawns.

◀ The forecourt of this Italian-inspired home in Southern California is bounded on one side by an arcade, which gives a feeling of enclosure and open space at the same time. The courtyard, designed by Carole McElwee, is in the classic quadripartite form with an octagonal pond recalling ancient garden design. Boxwood hedging, dark Italian cypress, and the olive tree repeat traditional mediterranean plantings. Paved, but porous, walking surfaces are appropriate for the climate. The tinkling sound of water falling into the basin beckons you to linger in this classic outdoor room.

▲ High walls surrounded the earliest *hortus conclusus*, or enclosed garden, for protection. At Villa le Balze in the hills above Florence, Italy, landscape architect Cecil Pinsent and his partner, Geoffrey Scott, devised just such a space off the library. By the 1920s high-walled protection was no longer needed, but the tradition had become part of the new Italianate fashion. Through this window in the wall one can look out over the magnificent view of the Arno valley, but only if close to the window. This kind of surprise is a special feature of a walled garden.

◀ The very last patio at the foot of the garden at Casa del Herrero overlooks what once was the cactus garden and the view to the sea before the trees below grew too high. The enclosing walls, capped with blue and yellow tiles, and the matching oil jars serve as a civilizing contrast to the wildness beyond. Owner Mr. George Fox Steedman, a skilled blacksmith and artisan, crafted most of the ornamental details for the house and garden. The exquisite wrought-iron gate, with its metal balusters, was designed by him and executed in his workshop.

▲ If hedges are walls for a garden, these towering hedges at La Casella in southern France could certainly be battlements. Formed of tightly sheared cypress, they lead you through a dark passage, around a corner, and down these graceful steps. Brushing past tobira (*Pittosporum tobira*), with its creamy white flowers smelling of orange blossoms, and silvery gray santolina (*Santolina chamaecyparissus*), you find yourself on the bright, sun-filled terrace below. It is a stunning transition from one garden room to another.

Arcaded interior courtyards, open to the sky, have been traditional in Mediterranean Spain since the tenth-century Muslim conquest. Can Sureda, in the heart of Palma, Majorca, maintains that tradition, even though it was built much later. The rectangular patio is divided into six spaces, and exquisite basket-handle arches atop red marble columns support the loggia. Pots of cast-iron plant *(Aspidistra elatior)* thrive in the open air of this typical eighteenth-century Majorcan Baroque townhouse.

▲ Güell Park outside of Barcelona is famous the world over because of its design by Spanish architect, and Barcelona's favorite son, Antonio Gaudí. This surreal, undulating bench, for which he used found pieces of stone, broken tile, and pottery, was designed in colorful waves to recall the tile of Hispano-Moorish tradition. Gaudí developed curving elevated roads and terraces to avoid cutting into the natural slopes of the hills, and he always planted with native plants—nearly a century ahead of today's ecological awareness.

▲ In another area of Güell Park the walkway, balustrade, and supports look as if they emerged like some fungal growth from the earth. Gaudí's enduring interest in ancient architecture is evident from the resemblance here to Roman aqueducts. But, instead of precise Roman engineering, a bizarre slant is given to the supports, which now resemble weight-bearing human legs. The vents look like so many worm holes, and the whole is encrusted with bulbous stones. The entire park, with its outrageous design attitude, has delighted the public for one hundred years.

◀ An outdoor fireplace warms and brightens the interior patio at La Casa Pacifica, above the beach in San Clemente, California. Built in 1926–27 for H. Hamilton Cotton, a banker, financier, and developer, the house became more famous in 1969, when it was bought by President and Mrs. Nixon, who named it La Casa Pacifica, the House of Peace. Overlooking one of the most important surfing beaches in Southern California, the gracious Spanish style house was so constantly in use during his presidency that it was dubbed "the Western White House." This very patio, with its outdoor fireplace and strong mediterranean style, has welcomed world leaders, U.S. Cabinet officers, senior White House staff, leaders of industry, returned Vietnam prisoners of war, and even astronauts.

◀ Several hedged passages and doorways open into this outdoor anteroom. Furnished with antique rusticated cement chairs and a table, this graveled space serves as a vestibule before you mount the steps at right onto a wide porch. The old urn is decorated with seashells, imparting a visual sense of place for this coastal California garden while recalling the decorative use of shells in Mediterranean gardens of long past. Pots of *fraise du bois (Fragaria vesca)* give you something to nibble as you pause here before exploring the rest of the garden.

Outdoor living is delightfully appealing on the rear patio of this French-inspired house in Santa Barbara, California. Its formal design is augmented by buns of potted boxwood and Italian cypress. Informal groups of pots with vines, variegated shrubs, and succulents soften the corners. Native Carmel creeper *(Ceanothus griseus horizontalis)* tumbles over a low wall in the foreground.

◄ The lazy atmosphere of this gracious old summer house is enhanced by the vining fern asparagus *(Asparagus setaceus)* that meanders over the doorway and onto the roof. A hedge of jade plant *(Crassula ovata)*, pots of ivy, and clipped boxwood sit on a gravel "lawn," completing a low-maintenance picture that requires little summer water. The row of scallop shells over the door evokes the charm of an old-fashioned garden, well loved and well used.

▶ A fireplace warms this new patio above Laguna Beach, California, on a typical cool evening—an invitation to stay up late. Creeping fig *(Ficus pumila)* softens the chimney, which is flanked on the left by coast rosemary *(Westringia fruticosa)* and on the right by the Australian willow *(Geijera parviflora)*. Container plantings are part of the outdoor furnishings, adding lushness and fragrance. Reliable iceberg roses, trained as standards, rise from pots spilling with sweet alyssum, creeping thyme, and white pansies. The basket is filled with continuous flowering white *Sutera cordata*, white ageratum, variegated *Vinca minor*, and ivy.

▲ Like a piece of garden sculpture that one stands in, this whimsical wrought-iron shower enclosure disguises the copper tubing that delivers the water from overhead. Korean grass *(Zoysia tenuifolia)* is soft under bare feet, and black-eyed Susan vine *(Thunbergia alata)* twines toward the top. This reliable summer bloomer has black-centered orange flowers, takes sun or light shade, and will soon veil the whole structure in a tangle of orange and green.

◀ Outdoor living is at its most inviting on this Southern California patio. Sumptuously furnished, as if indoors, the outdoor room is shaded by a wisteria-covered *ramada*, and the rattan-looking furniture is completely weatherproof. The 1920s Andalusian style farmhouse and its garden have been lovingly restored by its owners, George Martin and Jim Watterson.

MEDITERRANEAN STYLE

GARDEN ELEMENTS & DETAILS

◀ The remarkable Orange Garden at La Landriana, near Anzio, on the west coast of Italy, was conceived by one of that country's most important postwar gardeners, Lavinia Taverna. It was originally designed as a rose garden by the great Russell Paige. Madame Taverna kept the basic layout, but reinvented its design as a clipped, green, multilayered composition. Topmost are the naturally round-headed Norway maples *(Acer platanoides* 'Globosum'*).* Perfectly clipped sour oranges ('Bouquet de Fleurs') compose the next layer, and African box *(Myrsine africana)* is being trained into balls under them. The garden floor is filling in with a carpet of blue star creeper *(Pratia pedunculata)* and golden moneywort *(Lysimachia nummularia* 'Aurea'*).*

Elements and details are the motifs, harmonies, arpeggios, cadenzas, and trills that make a garden sing. Together with plants, it's the patios and paths, terraces and trellises, pergolas and paving, groves and gates, arches and alleés, hedges and walls that write the music and compose a garden. Both music and gardens can be serene or tumultuous, sweet or dramatic, depending on the chosen notes and their combinations.

Although we compare garden making to music or fine art, it alone is an art of three dimensions and five senses. Most of its components change constantly, depending on the weather, the seasons, and the involvement of the gardener. Thus it is music making with a modulating scale, a shifting rhythm, an occasional empty silence, or a raucous cacophony. Truly a wild thing, the garden must have architectural elements and structure to hold it all together.

Many of these elements and features are not unique to the mediterranean style, and this is because garden designers have always been quick to appropriate a good idea. However, garden-making began around the Mediterranean, not in England as many people believe. These ideas and elements were first devised to contend with Mediterranean climate conditions and the needs of those who lived in that region.

The use of formal geometry and axial design in gardens goes back to the ancient Greeks. They believed that all existence could be logically ordered, and that humans could control and balance the chaos of the natural world. Later, the Islamic religious belief that perfect symmetry and shape represented paradise served to reinforce the notion of perfect geometric gardens. For hundreds of years, it was thought that this was the only way to bring spiritual harmony and rational order to one's personal existence. Today's gardens are more often informal in design, with gently curving lines, soft shapes, and naturally growing plants. However, formal axial design and rigidly clipped plants still have the power to evoke tranquility through order.

Sheared evergreen shrubs with small to medium-size leaves and short internodes have long been used to make living garden walls called hedges, but they are also used to create clipped designs and simple architectural forms within a garden. Plants such as cypress, yew, laurel, bay, myrtle, boxwood, rosemary, and santolina have traditionally been shaped into tall fingers, short cones, lollipops, balls, and boxes. But other, more recently introduced plants are also useful for these simple topiary shapes. Among them are: *Pittosporum tenuifolium,* bush germander *(Teucrium fruticans),* Pacific wax myrtle *(Myrica californica),* African boxwood *(Myrsine africana),* variegated Italian buckthorn

(Rhamnus alaternus 'Variegata'*),* coffeeberry *(R. californica),* coast rosemary *(Westringia fruticosa),* and Australian fuchsias *(Correa* species). Solid, clipped evergreen forms are particularly important to a mediterranean garden during the cool, rainy winter and the long, hot sleep of summer when not much else is blooming or performing.

Colors in a mediterranean garden are usually the colors of the local earth. Stone, clay, or adobe is used for walls and structures, but these can also be painted. Interestingly, the paints are sometimes in the colors of food: tomato, pumpkin, squash, eggplant, apricot, peachy pink, even milky blue. In some mediterranean regions, houses and garden structures are traditionally whitewashed to deflect the heat instead of absorbing it. Mediterranean light is clear, bright, and sometimes dazzling. So flowering colors chosen for a garden in this climate need to be vibrant, like those of French or Italian faience, rather than the soft, polite colors of English china.

The practice of decorating living spaces with mosaic goes far back into Mediterranean history. Even before tile and marble were used, artistic floor designs were created using smooth water-worn beach and river pebbles of subtle color variations. Called pebble mosaic, this decorative art was perfected in ancient Greece by the late fourth century B.C. Magnificent floors, depicting graceful mythological scenes rendered in fine detail, are still being uncovered in modern archeological digs.

Because of the fascination with classical Greece, the art of pebble mosaic enjoyed a revival during the Italian Renaissance. Many of the surviving gardens from the period possess extraordinary pavings. Pebble mosaic, as well as other mosaic work, is enjoying a revival today, particularly along the Mediterranean coast. Whether in simple geometric designs or swirling abstract patterns, these pavings of water-polished stones sound an appropriate chord of earthiness in the sun-drenched style.

We think of Spain and Portugal as the origin of decorative tile making, when actually the very name for it, *azulejo*, comes from the Arabic *zulejo,* meaning "burnt stone." Centuries ago, the Arabs of the eastern Mediterranean perfected the process of baking clay squares in ovens or under the heat of the fierce sun, then decorating them with colored glazes before rebaking. The art form spread as Islamic civilization moved west. *Azulejo* made a perfect decorative surface—colorful, cool, clean, and durable. Used to surface walls and benches, and to line fountains and water rills, these tiles had become an important garden tradition by the time the Moors invaded southern Spain.

In the thirteenth century, the Moors were driven out of Spain, but *azulejo* remained, and the process made its way into Portugal, where artisans were free to depict the previously prohibited human and animal figures. With an expanded color palette, they produced composite pictures made up of several tiles, and Portugal became world renowned for its decorative tile. Today, tile is produced everywhere, and it comes in many different styles. But even now, when tiles are used in a garden, a mediterranean theme resounds.

Another recurring motif in the garden is the use of terra cotta—not only for roofs and floors, but for ornamentation and containers. In a mediterranean climate terra cotta can be left outside year round with no danger of damage. And the color of terra cotta can range from a deep, rich reddish brown to a pale putty-tan, depending on the color of the clay soil where the bowls, pots, and jars are made.

Clay is probably the oldest building material in the world—

A soft, rounded form of boxwood topiary sets off the severe stone architecture of the north facade at Villa Chigi Cetinale. This side of the dwelling, built in the Baroque style during the seventeenth century, is dominated by a massive staircase to the *piano nobile*. The rose Madame Alfred Carrière wantonly clings to the Italian stone balusters. Purchased in 1977 and since restored by Lord Lambton, the villa now displays a definite English overlay.

▲ Topiary can be simple and austere, as well as cute and frivolous. The tradition of clipped greenery goes back a long time in garden history and will probably continue, going in and out of fashion like many other garden elements. At Jas Crema, a whimsical doughnut is shaped out of the Mediterranean native bush germander *(Teucrium fruticans)*, forming a ring around the tree trunk.

▶ The dramatic entrance to Le Domaine du Vignole exemplifies the visual power of plant form. The proportional scale of the large sheared Italian cypress to the low balls of gray santolina focuses attention toward the entry court. Landscape architect Jean Mus says he never works from plans, but assembles all his ingredients like a chef, then creates his compositions in situ. Without relying on color, he creates drama from a plant palette limited to drought-tolerant Mediterranean natives. The twenty-five-year-old garden, north of Cannes in southern France, only gains in grace as it ages.

whole cities were made of it in ancient times. Abundant and easily worked, clay was suitable for making tiles, pots, bowls, jars, and ewers for both household and commercial use. Over the centuries, terra cotta, which means "baked earth," replaced unfired clay because it was stronger and had better resistance to weather.

Terra-cotta containers are still manufactured in the Basque regions of Spain; in Anduze, Southern France; in Impruneta, Italy; and on the Greek island of Crete. However, there are fewer and fewer artisans who still hand throw and fire pots by the old methods because it is both laborious and highly skilled work.

Iron has always been abundant in nature, but in an impure form. Though it was known to be strong, it was brittle. Early blacksmiths eventually learned that iron had to be heated and hammered again and again to expel the carbon and impurities that made it so easily broken. Knowledge of the secrets of refining, the tools, and the skill to use them gave these artisans both prestige and power in an age when strong weapons were of utmost importance. In alliance with the great god Vulcan, the Roman blacksmith was thought to possess magical powers, enabling him to control the hardest metal then known to man.

Wrought iron, made and refined in charcoal fires, first flourished as a decorative art form in the Middle Ages, when it was utilized to adorn and embellish the great cathedrals. Although the blacksmith no longer enjoys the reverence he once commanded, today his work graces our homes and gardens with objects both useful and beautiful. Iron furniture and fixtures, banisters and doors, fences and gates, even candle holders and other ornamental objects are important elements in the mediterranean garden.

Food is rarely out of mind and seldom out of sight in a sun-drenched garden. So important to the Mediterranean way of life, the growing of food is a year-round activity, and it is considered to be just as, if not more, beautiful than ornamental growing. Even the smallest modern gardens have vegetables and fruit trees, which are not hidden behind the garage as in many American gardens, but up close to the house, and decoratively combined with flowers and herbs.

▶ Near the entrance of the modern Italian garden at Valle Pinciole, a battery of shrubs sheared into balls look as if they are rolling down the slope, soon to bounce over the wattle fence onto the drive. Made from several different evergreen shrubs of varying sizes, colors, and textures, this bed of simple topiary never fails to command a double take and a smile. Here are Chinese holly (Ilex cornuta), yaupon (I. vomitoria), English laurel (Prunus laurocerasus), Portugal laurel (P. lusitanica), tobira (Pittosporum tobira), English yew (Taxus baccata), Hinoki false cypress (Chamaecyparis obtusa), oriental arborvitae (Thuja orientalis), myrtle (Myrtus communis), Luma apiculata, and African boxwood (Myrsine africana). In this part of Italy with its clay soils, wattle fencing is successfully used as a retaining wall.

Early Roman frescoes show women working in the *hortus,* close to the dwelling, while their children play nearby. Grains such as wheat and barley were grown in these gardens, as well as edible greens, like cabbage and kale. Asparagus, parsley, rue, capers, fennel, parsnips, mustard, and samphire were all grown in this convenient enclosed space called the *hortus.*

This garden model, spread by the Romans throughout the then-known world, has persisted to the present day. In southern Europe it is common practice to mix food-producing plants with flowering, scented, and herbal plants—not informally like in an English border, but in rows like in planting fields. The traditional agricultural geometry, enhanced by scent and ornament, has become a signature of modern mediterranean style gardens as well.

◀ This classic parterre epitomizes how hedges can be used as architectural elements. Done in a severe geometric style, this is one of the newest gardens at Château Ansouis near Aix-en-Provence, France. Located behind the battlements of this tenth-century castle, the boxwood parterre is designed to be looked down on from the living quarters. But it can also be walked through, as a kind of labyrinth.

▶ Superb boxwood parterres at Villa Lante embellish the lower level of this terraced garden, designed to trace the philosophical development of man. It represents what was then, in the modern age of Renaissance Italy, the humanist philosophy of man's dominion over nature. The Humanists believed God gave mankind the right and the ability to tame nature, to craft and shape it to human needs, and, in so doing, to create art. The precision of these clipped parterres magnificently illustrates humanity's quest to tame nature.

▶ This arresting vista extends across several descending terraces in the garden at La Casella. From this vantage point at the top terrace, one looks between two pilasters topped with stone fruit baskets to the next terrace, across a small spout of water edged with boxwood and surrounded by lavender and standard roses to the next, perfectly clipped boxwood buns and more lavender, and then to the lowest level, with its stone urn backed by the dark forms of Italian cypress. The axial view, revealing multiple levels in space, becomes an ingenious device to lure one into the garden.

▲ An amusing topiary clipped in the shape of a spiral terebra shell sits near the tool house at La Casella. Trained from a variegated form of New Zealand kohuhu *(Pittosporum tenuifolium)*, the large, bright twist is a perfect foil for the relaxed and natural growth of the surrounding trees and shrubs. The spring bloom of the Judas tree *(Cercis siliquastrum)* lights up the background, as this delightfully innovative garden runs seamlessly into the landscape.

▶ The chiaroscuro effect at the forecourt and entry at Lotusland, in Santa Barbara, California, is heightened by the flamboyance of fantastic planting. Aging euphorbias loom at the windows, and mature treelike cacti guard the doors, while golden barrel cacti look as if they tumble about underneath. This idiosyncratic garden, created in the 1940s by Polish opera singer Madame Ganna Walska, dramatically proves that there are no right ways in gardening, only alternatives.

One of the most arresting design elements at Villa Noailles, near Grasse, is this dark portico of sculpted boxwood. Really only a facade, it is fashioned to look like a triumphal arch, through which one can wander to the lily pool. At the base of its curving hedge banisters, an ancient gray santolina *(Santolina chamaecyparissus)* spills into the sunken garden below. Considered the most imposing piece of garden architecture in the south of France, it perfectly fits the definition of a garden folly.

▲ At El Laberinto d'Horta, a municipal park outside Barcelona, the eighteenth-century mansion and garden are now open to the public. From its neoclassical pavilion, one looks out over radiating rows of hedges to a pool with crossing jets of water. Beyond is the famous cypress maze, a popular garden feature of that era, which must have entertained and mystified garden guests for hours.

▶ (Overleaf) At the far side of the broad lawn at Lotusland is one of the most theatrical plantings in a garden known for dramatic excesses. Blue agave *(Agave americana),* their sinuous leaves reaching out like ballerinas' arms, writhe in front of a group of stealthy-looking blue yucca *(Yucca rigida),* their persistent, spent leaves wrapped like overcoats against the wind.

◀ A mediterranean style meadow garden, complete with a mown path, is hidden behind the streetside fence in this Southern California garden. It is planted with drought-tolerant buffalo grass *(Buchloe dactyloides)*, red valerian *(Centranthus ruber)*, and hundreds of spring-blooming mediterranean-climate bulbs. Under the light shade of the olive and fruit trees, the meadow has naturalized into a seasonal cycle of its own. Winter rains bring on green growth and spring bloom; then, as the summer progresses, bulb foliage yellows and dies back, and the valerian is cut back to keep it from self-seeding. Finally, in autumn, the grass turns less green, more straw.

▶ The meadow garden at Villa Noailles near Grasse is actually one of seven old, stone-walled terraces with their original olive trees. Below the olives, this terrace has been planted with native Mediterranean grasses and wild flowers. Underneath sprout both wild and rare bulbs that have naturalized; they bloom in white, cream, gold, and pink at different times throughout the year. Meadow gardens are a favorite with everyone, perhaps because their rural simplicity and casual charm contrast with the more intensely cultivated parts of the garden.

◀ Architect Cecil Pinsent felt strongly that to be true to the Italian Renaissance style, plants and flowers must be only supporting elements to the clipped greenery and hard stone architecture of each space. Gardens should be roomlike, some open and some completely enclosed, and each room should retain its essential character in winter, without colorful leaves and flowers, as well as in summer. This lower garden at Villa le Balze is a good example of that conviction. Its simple green design never competes with its authentic Renaissance neighbor, the Villa Medici, or the view of the Arno valley just beyond the balustrade.

The small, graceful Villa Chigi Cetinale is nestled in the rolling hills near Sienna. Carlo Fontana, the great Baroque artist and architect, created a structure of exquisite beauty, perfectly sited along axial lines. The garden in the forecourt reflects that same elegant simplicity, with only clipped greenery, lemons in *tondo,* and two stone statues. Everything is composed to frame and enhance the dwelling, as if it were a jewel set in a mounting.

For hundreds of years in Italy, olive oil was transported and stored in terra-cotta containers like this one, called *orchi*. Thrown by hand and roughly modeled after Greek and Roman amphorae, they were wide and round below, with a narrower opening at the top. These containers were designed to be sunk into the ground in order to keep the oil cool, so they had handles and some kind of scoring or ridge around the body to mark how deep to sink them. When modern ceramic and glass containers appeared, these terra-cotta urns were thrown out. Some exquisitely beautiful examples, signed and embellished with the owners' crests, can still be found idly decorating old Italian villa gardens. Today copies are made, and a modern mediterranean style garden feels incomplete without its reminder of the olive and its "Golden Liquid, gift of the gods."

▲ Until just recently, the definition of a mediterranean-climate region was anywhere the olive tree grew. Indeed, olives have been a major crop around the Mediterranean for more than ten thousand years. Considered a gift from the gods by ancient Greeks, the tree became a symbol of peace, wisdom, and triumph. It was sacred to Athena, who wore an olive wreath on her helmet and carried an amphora of olive oil, and centuries of Olympic champions were crowned with olive leaves. Called "that Golden Liquid" by Homer, the oil has always been prized for its health-giving benefits, as well as its distinctive flavor.

▶ A *provençal potager* is intimate, flowerful, and close to the kitchen door. Even at the large châteaux in the south of France ornamental planting is mixed with food production, and the garden is placed near the dwelling. Historically, people had to make the most of poor soil and limited water, so it was easier if the garden was close at hand. They could enrich the soil with kitchen scraps and irrigate with used water. Today, this mediterranean tradition continues.

◀ In Provence, where agriculture for profit is carried out on a small scale, the plants grown for food have never been separated from those grown for ornamentation. The modern garden at the winery of Château Val Joanis, near Pertuis, carries on that strong tradition. Beds of gourmet beans are edged with lavender, and the lovage is fronted with a hedge of golden yew. The main walks are edged with balls of boxwood. Columns of Italian cypress and slender cones of yew punctuate the garden throughout.

◀ The kitchen garden at Casa del Herrero in Santa Barbara, California, has been restored and turned into an herb garden, laid out in a pleasing quadripartite design. Outer beds are further divided into four, each with a clipped bay topiary, and the whole is enclosed with white walls. You can look out to the orchard below over the low pergola wall; and the gate, exquisitely fashioned from wrought iron, leads to a rose garden. Against the far wall is an unusual pomegranate, carefully espaliered to splay against the flat surface.

▸ A California country kitchen garden, complete with artichokes and tomatoes, is fenced in with natural wood branches and entered through a charming, bentwood gate. Golden hop *(Humulus lupulus* 'Aureus'*)* competes with nasturtiums for a place on the tuteur and archway. Pink breath of heaven *(Coleonema pulchrum)*, with its sweet fragrance, begs to be brushed as you pass by.

◀ Beans climbing their supports are a sculptural element in this *potager*, only steps away from the kitchen through a gate in the rose-covered wall. Lavender *(Lavandula X intermedia)*, called *lavandin* in Provence, is planted in crop rows between the vegetables. Fragrant and beautiful, it increases bee activity, and has been a tradition in kitchen gardens for hundreds of years.

▶ This superb little *potager* has culinary herbs in the central beds, and tomatoes and beans planted at the outer edges. The young bay tree in the center is planted in a pot so it will not outgrow its space. The biscuit-beige gravel blends in with the color of the stone walls.

▲ A pleasure in any mediterranean-climate garden, where lemons can be grown outside year round, is the lemon pergola. At once beautiful and useful, the structure must be open enough for the fruit to hang through yet strong enough to support the laden branches. At Lotusland, young 'Eureka' lemon trees were planted at each post and trained up by tying, then pruning off outward branches. When they reached the top, some side branches were retained, while others were pulled over and tied to the joists. In hot summer conditions, the trunks of lemon trees should be whitewashed to protect them from sunburn.

Food and flowers in a Mediterranean street market are delights for the eye as much as the palate. Beauty and freshness are equally valued, so fruit, vegetables, and herbs are offered only in season. Clockwise from top left: purple artichokes, herbs, strawberries, squashes, pomegranates, potpourri

▶ The most famous axial vista in all of Italy is from the north facade at Villa Chigi Cetinale. Down a broad grassy *viale*, between towering cypress, brick piers, and more cypress, across a clearing, and up the steep steps of the Scala Santa to the hermitage at the crest of the hill, this view produces an astonishing illusion of distance and grandeur. Its creator, the seventeenth-century architect Carlo Fontana, was able to accomplish this amazing effect with a property considered small for its time.

▼ At Clos du Peyronnet above the French Riviera, the garden steps up a steep slope behind the house, on narrow terraces that are retained with fine stone walls. On this terrace, planted with dwarf fruit trees, a one-person path runs between stone arches. The stonework echoes the bare, stony face of the mountain beyond and ties the highly cultivated garden to its landscape. The path is planted with common bearded iris on both sides. The elongated perspective makes the garden appear larger than it really is.

▶ Architect Michelozzo Michelozzi built this impressive retaining wall to hold back the upper terrace at the fifteenth-century Villa Medici—what a remarkable engineering feat for its time. Cosimo the Elder wanted a villa from which he could look down on all of Florence, so the site had to be carved out of the rocks of Fiesole above. Visible from the city below, the wall must have been, as it was intended, an everyday reminder of the power and influence this mighty family possessed. Today it sprouts vines and self-sown seedlings, softening its austerity so much that it has been called a "hanging garden."

▲ From the auto court in the modern Italian garden at Villa Massai, one looks across to the former entry between a pair of aged Italian cypress. Over the past twenty years, two talented Americans, Gil Cohen and Paul Gervais, have labored to rescue and re-create this garden honoring the spirit of Renaissance Tuscany. Beds of clipped greenery are edged with tiny hedges of gray santolina. Yews *(Taxus baccata)*, clipped in the form of pointed cones, fill the Italian terra-cotta pots on the near side. Potted lemon trees and the hedged *viale* provide a traditional countenance to the forecourt.

◀ From the lowest level at Villa Lante, one can see the magnificent axial perspective given this garden by its designer, Giacomo Barozzi da Vignola, a sixteenth-century Italian scholar, artist, philosopher, and architect. Through the lower parterre, over the Fountain of the Moors, past the perfectly square, twin *casini*, and up to the second terrace with its Fountain of the Lights, one senses the mirrorlike duality of the symmetrical design. Ancient plane trees still grace this terrace; above, oaks and holly are skillfully worked into the garden plan, making Villa Lante as rich in shade as it is in water.

◀ Above the monumental retaining wall at Villa Medici, the upper terrace holds the handsome early Renaissance style house, noted for its simplicity and sturdy construction. Featuring two aged empress trees *(Paulownia tomentosa)* and lined with potted lemons, the terrace is an outdoor extension of the dwelling and ties it to the landscape by mirroring the structure's classic proportions. Five hundred years ago, Lorenzo de Medici strolled along this very parapet, deep in philosophical discussions with famed artists, scholars, and members of his Platonic Society. Today, with its unifying pots of red geraniums, the garden represents everything to which the mediterranean style aspires.

▶ Villa di Geggiano, overlooking Sienna, Italy, has been in the same family since 1527, and is still supported by its vineyards and olive groves. The magnificent front facade looks out onto a graveled forecourt that is approached from a long narrow drive colonnaded with ancient Italian cypress. Lemon trees, potted in traditional, handmade *tondo,* are mounted for the summer on special stone plinths, called *sotto conche,* and carefully wheeled into the *limonaia* for winter protection.

▶ (Overleaf) Below the grand pergola at La Casella, this narrow terrace is designed to be looked down upon, so it has been completely paved in pebble mosaic. This ancient art, called *calades* in France, uses smooth, round stones of different colors to form decorative patterns. It is a functional walking surface as well as a beautiful garden feature.

▲ An antique French laundry pot is a major focal point at a bend in this path. Frothing at its mouth is the gray South African native licorice plant *(Helichrysum petiolare)*, which smells of licorice in the sun. Self-seeding vitti-dinia or Mexican daisy *(Erigeron karvinskiana)* has moved in around the base, where it finds collected moisture. A delightful garden orna-ment, the pot has been carefully mended with wire, only adding to its charm.

▶ One of the most handsome *calades* in southern France is in the forecourt of Villa Noailles near Grasse. The pattern of this pebble mosaic is made by laying the water-polished stones on their sides in various configurations. Although the stones are the same color and set in cement, moss has filled in the joints between them, setting off their design to advantage. The practice of using sea and river pebbles to decorate floors dates from the ancient Greek civilization that occupied the eastern Mediterranean and has been used in dwellings and gardens ever since.

▲ Paving with loose gravel or stone chips, as in this entry court at Château Ansouis in the Luberon, France, is one of the best ways to cover a flat area in a mediterranean garden. The surface remains permeable and allows what rain does fall to penetrate rather than run off. The courtyard is ornamented only with elegantly simple stone benches and Anduze urns in front of a boxwood hedge, framing and enhancing the magnificent view over the Durance Gap in a way that more intricate plantings could never do.

▶ The warm squash color of the dwelling at Villa le Balze is set off by traditional gray stone trim. Clipped boxwood in symmetrically placed pots complete the mediterranean picture.

▼ A grapevine reaches across the lintel of a doorway in the small *village perche* of Roussillon, softening the stony facade. The burnt umber color of the local stones and clay gives the *provençal* village its fame and supplies the art world with natural pigments. These earthy tones have become so traditional in Mediterranean gardens that garden makers in other countries are staining their cement with iron oxide to give it a similar effect.

◀ Peering through the Baroque gate at Villa Aurelia, one has a view into the treetops and over the city of Rome. This lovely eighteenth-century wrought-iron gate is flanked by hanging lamps that once burned olive oil. The warm pumpkin-colored walls are quintessentially Mediterranean. Villa Aurelia was built right on top of ancient Roman defensive walls, and the remnants are still visible as one descends stairs into the steep garden below.

▲ A tumult of sizzling red ivy geranium (*Pelargonium peltatum*) tumbles from the iron window casing at the entrance to Casa del Herrero. Foundry mogul George F. Steedman named his estate "house of the blacksmith," but he was far from a humble blacksmith. Every wrought-iron detail was made in his home workshop, and every window grille is different, designed by Steedman from Spanish motifs.

◀ In Barcelona, a tiny balcony with a graceful wrought-iron railing hangs over a small garden.

◀ Greenery wreathes the doorway at Villa Massai by means of an ingenious frame of light wire fastened to the wall. Evergreen wire vine *(Muehlenbeckia complexa)* is being carefully trained to cover the structure.

▼ A handsome wrought-iron gate swings open at the entrance to this *provençal* garden, Mas Oiseau, above Grasse.

▶ Decorated with handmade tile medallions, this window demonstrates the trend of modernist experimentation using traditional materials that occurred in Barcelona at the turn of the twentieth century.

◀ A delicate wrought-iron gate leads from one part of the garden to another at La Mortola, the Hanbury Botanical Garden, on the Italian Riviera. The lacy iron filigree suggests it was made in the early twentieth century, during the time when Lady Dorothy Hanbury sought to turn what was an unruly collection of plants into a genuine garden. When well placed in a garden, fine wrought-iron work is as important as decorative sculpture.

▶ (Overleaf) The massive stairs that descend from the rear terrace at Le Domaine du Vignole are a dominating architectural statement. To soften the austerity, landscape architect Jean Mus dribbled a line of pots down the center, where no one walks anyway. Planted with native boxwood *(Buxus sempervirens)* and santolina *(Santolina chamaecyparissus)*, the pots repeat the plantings at the sides and blend the stairway into the garden. Four lovely Anduze pots at the corners contain pink flowering ivy geraniums *(Pelargonium peltatum)*.

One of the newer additions to Lotusland, the Australian Garden is in keeping with the style set by its flamboyant owner, right down to the blue glass slag scattered between the bricks. Designed by landscape architect Sydney Baumgartner, the garden is completely planted with Australian natives. Embracing the pergola, Australian tea trees (*Leptospermum laevigatum*) are precisely pruned and trained to espalier over the top. The underplanting is Australian fuchsia (*Correa* 'Dusky Bells' and *C.* 'Ivory Bells'), backed by silvery gray *Plectranthus argentatus*. In the foreground are the dark, ribbed leaves of spear lily (*Doryanthes palmeri*), which may bloom only once in fifteen years.

Narrow steps, their risers embellished with *azulejos*, create a striking reminder of Spain in a California garden. The stark winter form of tropical Mexican plumeria (*Plumeria rubra*) looks to trap anyone who steps onto the landing. The tree's incredibly fragrant flowers typically come before its leaves emerge.

From the living room at Casa del Herrero, one looks across the Spanish Patio toward the *exedra*. Built in the 1930s, sometime after the rest of the garden, it makes a perfect terminus for the eastern vista. The blue, yellow, and white *azulejo* composite surrounded by tiled benches with geometric designs and stylized flowers adds a Hispano-Moorish flavor to this California garden.

At Casa del Herrero, an outdoor sink is covered with tile in the *azulejo* style of Moorish Spain. Only arabesque or geometric designs were permitted on this early form of tile, and authentic reproductions, such as these from Tunis, adhere to that tradition.

GREAT PLANTS, INSPIRED PLANTINGS

Summertime in a mediterranean garden is incomplete without the scent of lavender clinging to your legs—it is that essential. Native to the northern side of the Mediterranean Sea, lavender grows on poor, rocky soil in mountainous regions. The genus *Lavandula* and all its species have grown wild and been cultivated by man for more than two thousand years. A plant that has adapted over time to the challenges of a hard life, lavender needs sun-drenched, poor, well-drained soil and little, if any, water during the summer. Grown thus, it remains tight and dignified, but given lush and rosy conditions it soon loses its composure.

Despite popular misconceptions, today's garden makers have a huge palette of plants from which to choose when composing a sun-drenched garden. Although summer-dry gardens are reputed to be made of only prickly and dead-looking plants, nothing could be further from the truth. The five mediterranean-climate areas around the world make up only two percent of the earth's land surface but produce among them a vast repertoire of garden-worthy plants. Better yet, many other species from temperate and subtropical regions are also tolerant of arid summer conditions after they become established, increasing the choices for today's gardeners.

While most places in the world have rain on and off during the summer months, mediterranean climates almost never do. The significant olive, gray, and silver tones of a mediterranean garden's foliage are due to these plants' survival adaptations to summer drought. Other mediterranean plants have a protective waxy coating or a silky surface that reflects sunlight. On certain days, when the light is right, plants such as olives, mastic/lentisc *(Pistacia lentiscus)*, Pacific wax myrtle *(Myrica californica)*, and Ceanothus species seem to shimmer.

147

Still others like lavenders, artemisias, westringias, and leucospermums shine because of the tiny reflective hairs on their leaves. This luminescence gives the garden a sparkling, almost magical atmosphere, especially if these plants are contrasted with those that have dark burgundy-bronze leaves, such as purple hop bush (*Dodonaea viscosa* 'Purpurea'), purple leaf grape (*Vitis vinifera* 'Purpurea'), purple smoke bush (*Cotinus coggygria* 'Royal Purple'), or purple fountain grass (*Pennisetum setaceum* 'Rubrum').

In addition, some mediterranean perennials have adapted to long, hot summers by becoming fuzzy, or downright woolly, such as *Verbascum olympicum, V. bombyciferum,* shrubby little *Ballota pseudodictamnus,* or the versatile *Plectranthus argentatus* that adapts to sun or shade. A few succulent plants develop a soft, white powdery surface, like *Dudleya brittonii,* and the wavy-edged *Cotyledon undulata*. In a sun-drenched garden, there's more to marvel at than just flower color.

For surprise and sculptural drama, nothing can compare to the world of cacti and succulents, from the large treelike euphorbias and wickedly spined agaves, down to intricate little sempervivums and echeveria, which mimic roses blooming right out of the ground. There is something for every size mediterranean garden in this plant group: beautiful blooming aloes, haworthias that look like octopuses, crassulas trained as hedges, yuccas that resemble star bursts, and aeonium rosettes bigger than dinner plates. Some succulents prefer shade. Many need not be grown in their own garden bed but can mingle happily with other drought-tolerant plants, like good guests at a party. Just one magnificent *Beschorneria yuccoides* can bring fascination and excitement to an otherwise dull gathering.

All species of plants were wild somewhere once, and many of those from mediterranean climates adapted a

dense, hummocky shape for survival. This low, mounding shape kept the plant from being torn by the occasional fierce winds typical of this climate and shaded its roots from the summer sun. Although they belong to different species and are known by various local names in these wide-flung regions, these plants share a similar shape and look. Aromatic and sometimes spiny, the low mounds look good in a garden setting. Early gardeners would seek them out and clip others to produce that tight, rounded form.

Today we see these hummocky plants in natural native gardens, as well as clipped into tight balls and buns in more formal gardens. Boxwood lavender, santolina, westringia, correa, cushion bush (*Calocephalus brownii*), African boxwood (*Myrsine africana*), plus certain California buckwheats, several different artemisias, and beach aster (*Erigeron glaucus*) varieties are just a few clipable and mounding examples that contribute to the mediterranean look.

Until recently, the only plants available to gardeners in mediterranean climates were some of the tough Mediterranean herbs, a few locally native plants, and a great many species and hybrids that are born and bred in cooler, moister climates. In addition, glossy magazines, books, television, and garden experts from other climates have long shaped our ideals of what is beautiful. They paraded before us luscious water-gulping gardens and praised sumptuous

Native *Iris germanica*, so familiar in Mediterranean area gardens, is known by several local names: orris, Florentine iris, *Fleur de Lis*, and van Gogh iris. Easy to naturalize in untended areas, the plant blooms with winter and spring rains, then retreats to underground rhizomes for the long summer dormancy.

flowering, water-needy species. Most of the time, the garden ideals these experts champion are ill-suited to the intense sunlight of the mediterranean climate, and are unachievable without endless irrigation and fertilization. A sweeping emerald lawn, English cottage flower borders, and year-round color are never quite attainable in mediterranean conditions.

There is good news. Contemporary plant hunters, innovative nurseries, and botanic gardens are seeking out, selecting, and introducing new species and handsome cultivars that thrive in winter-wet, summer-dry conditions. Several nurseries and mail-order houses offer plants from all five mediterranean climates. Thus it falls to gardeners to support this effort, rather than just continue to buy and plant the same old delphiniums and hybrid tea roses because they are familiar, or we have admired them in a gardening magazine. It is time to learn about and try climate-appropriate introductions.

It is also time to re-examine the notion of what a garden should look like in a mediterranean climate. Let's form our own garden models, our own ideals of beauty that emanate from the locale, soil, and weather. Let's take the time to appreciate the mediterranean environment's tawny beauty and earthy palette of olive green, gray, and gold.

Where better to look for design inspiration than the cradle of Western civilization around the Mediterranean Sea where styles, traditions, and elements have evolved through two thousand years of garden-making experience? In the Mediterranean region, stone, clay, and architecture have long worked together with evergreen plant form, mass, and texture to create the characteristic garden and landscape aesthetic. Plants grown in the area are native, summer-drought tolerant, and low-maintenance.

A discussion of the mediterranean garden is incomplete without mentioning the beautiful food-producing plants. After all, this climate has always been famous for its wine grapes, olives, figs, and citrus. The abundant fruits, vegetables, and herbs are prominently grown alongside ornamental plants—a practice based on longstanding traditions that are both practical and aesthetic. The new mediterranean garden can be both easy to care for and easy on our resources. It is a place to spend more time, a personal sanctuary where one is treated to a complete sensual experience—one of sight, sound, scent, touch, and taste.

▶ A semishade planting gets sun only until noon but still gives great color. In the background, the common heliotrope (Heliotropum arborescens) reliably blooms just about every day of the year in a mild climate. Vivid red alstromeria is woven through with coppery shrimp plant (Justicia brandegeeana) and serves to hold up the shrimp's lax stems. Evergreen alstromeria will bloom through the season if its spent stems are pulled out from the base.

◀ Rosy-colored seedpods follow the salmon-colored winter flowers on the treelike Aloe marlothii.

◀ Beneath the high umbrella of a Canary Island palm *(Phoenix canariensis)*, a throbbing crimson Bougainvillea 'San Diego Red' sprawls across the roof of the gatehouse at La Casa Pacifica. Below the wall, a mature tobira *(Pittosporum tobira)* is skirted with euphorbia *(Euphorbia characias wulfenii)* bearing its chubby chartreuse bloom heads. The modern additions to this California garden were designed by Lew Whitney of Roger's Gardens.

▶ Silvery gray and olive green are the signature colors of a sun-drenched garden. Deep borders planted under olive trees at Giardini della Landriana, show off the fine textures and subtle shades of gray in this most mediter-ranean of modern Italian gardens. Billowing out over the edge of the tufa walk, rockrose *(Cistus X pur-pureus)* hangs on to its last spring blooms. In front, the fine silvery foliage of lavender cotton *(Santolina chamaecyparissus)*, and behind, felty-leaved dusty miller *(Centaurea cineraria)* provide contrast, while the olive trees, symbol of Mediterranean life, spread their branches over all.

◀ Against a rough stone, the toothed, daggerlike leaves of soap aloe *(Aloe saponaria)* consort with the flat, round leaves of an *Aeonium* hybrid, creating a small, succulent moment that captures the essence of great planting design.

▼ With its wicked spines, yellow variegated *Agave americana* 'Marginata' makes a dramatic flourish wherever it is placed. The plant can spread to ten feet across before sending up a huge bloom stalk.

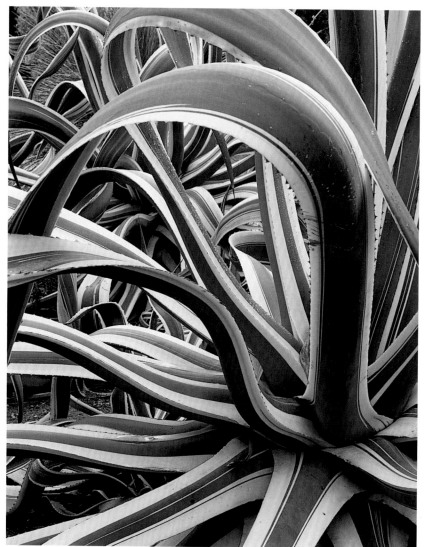

▲ Chocolate-bronze *Dyckia fosteriana* hybrid, a terrestrial bromeliad relative, stands in high relief against the pale, glaucous mosaic of *Echeveria elegans*, sometimes called Mexican gem.

◄ A delightful collection of succulents in antique and handmade containers garnish a corner of this patio. Outstanding among them is the book aloe (*Aloe plicatilis*), with its fleshy, stacked gray leaves. In front is a collection of fancy-leafed echeverias with sempervivum and a red-edged *Kalanchoe thrysiflora*. On the low blocks, a gray-leafed sedum (*Sedum sieboldii*) fills out the back pot, and a dwarf jade plant (*Crassula ovata*) shares a container with *Aloe brevifolia*. This talented gardener has found plants that will withstand her frequent absences and minimal watering, while retaining their good looks.

▶ (Overleaf) A dry garden composition at Lotusland in Santa Barbara, California, showcases tree euphorbias (*Euphorbia canariense*), night-blooming saguaro (*Carnegiea gigantea*), and golden barrel cacti (*Echinocactus grusonii*).

155

▲ Looming as high as the second-story windows, the famous giant, *Euphorbia ingens* var. *monstrosa*, kneels over on its knuckles to gain more support. Native to equatorial Africa, this monster is beautiful but possesses sharp spines and a caustic, poisonous sap.

◀ Rosy-flowered beaver tail cactus (*Opuntia basilaris*) provide a backdrop for yellow flowering bunny ears cactus (*O. microdasys*), so called because the new pads grow at the top of the old, resembling rabbits' ears.

159

◀ This unusual dry garden focuses on plant form and texture for its effect. Potted false sea onion *(Ornithogalum longibracteatum)*, with cascades of wavy foliage, appear to flow over the sides into a sea of foaming wire vine *(Muehlenbeckia axillaris)*, creating the impression of flowing water where there is none.

▼ Coast rosemary *(Westringia fruticosa)*, sheared to fat buns, line the tiled inner courtyard of this mediterranean style home. Trained to frame the seventeenth-century Portuguese *azulejo* composite, the white bougainvillea is trying to revert to pink, a habit for which it is notorious.

◀ An arresting streetside planting in the California garden of designer Carole McElwee is composed of tough, drought-resistant plants adapted to the mediterranean climate. It belies the common notion that these gardens can only look prickly, dry, and brown. In the foreground, white blooming Mexican evening primrose *(Oenothera speciosa* 'Alba'*)* grows next to clumping gray African daisy *(Arctotis acaulis* 'Magenta'*)*, in front of the fat chartreuse bloom heads of euphorbia *(Euphorbia characias wulfenii)*. Beyond the trailing prostrate rosemary *(Rosmarinus officinalis* 'Prostratus'*)*, purple everblooming Mexican bush sage *(Salvia leucantha)* arches over gray lavender cotton *(Santolina chamaecyparissus)* and verbena *(Verbena rigida)*. A clipped ball of Japanese boxwood *(Buxus microphylla japonica)* anchors each side of the driveway, while a dark hedge of purple hop bush *(Dodonaea viscosa* 'Purpurea'*)* forms a backdrop for silvery gray-olive foliage.

◀ Rub the leaves of this plant and you will understand why one of its common names is sandpaper vine. *Petrea volubilis*, also called queen's wreath, blooms heavily in late spring and lightly throughout the summer with soft clusters of lavender-blue wands. A frost-tender vine, easy to train and prune, it can lace up walls or cavort over an arch. It blooms best on hot roofs and south-facing walls.

◀ Large bowl-like golden blooms, which broadcast an elusive fragrance at night, are the attraction of this rampantly fast-growing cup-of-gold vine *(Solandra maxima)*.

◀ The toughness and adaptability of common wisteria have made it a familiar mediterranean-garden resident. Drought-tolerant and able to live to a great age, the vine becomes more interesting and beautiful as it matures. Every winter, while bare, the woody vine should be pruned and tied to fill its allotted space and freely drop its spring blooms.

◀ Looking like a row of specimens lined up on a museum shelf, these different cultivars of Italian cypress *(Cupressus sempervirens)* wait to be compared at the Cap Roig Botanic Garden, north of Barcelona.

◀ What was once a California lemon grove is now the site for a new mediterranean style house and garden. Nothing could be more appropriate than to keep portions of the citrus grove as part of the landscape. Well-trimmed and cared for, the Eureka lemon trees bear fruit year round and provide the new garden with its important sense of place.

▶ A row of lavendin *(Lavandula X intermedia)* is just beginning to send up its bloom spikes against the wall, and a green rosemary rug spreads under the olive tree. Tough and tolerant of dry soil, *Rosmarinus officinalis* 'Prostratus', set out from rooted cuttings spaced two feet apart, soon develops into a thick carpet. It should be sheared periodically from the very beginning to keep the growth dense and tight.

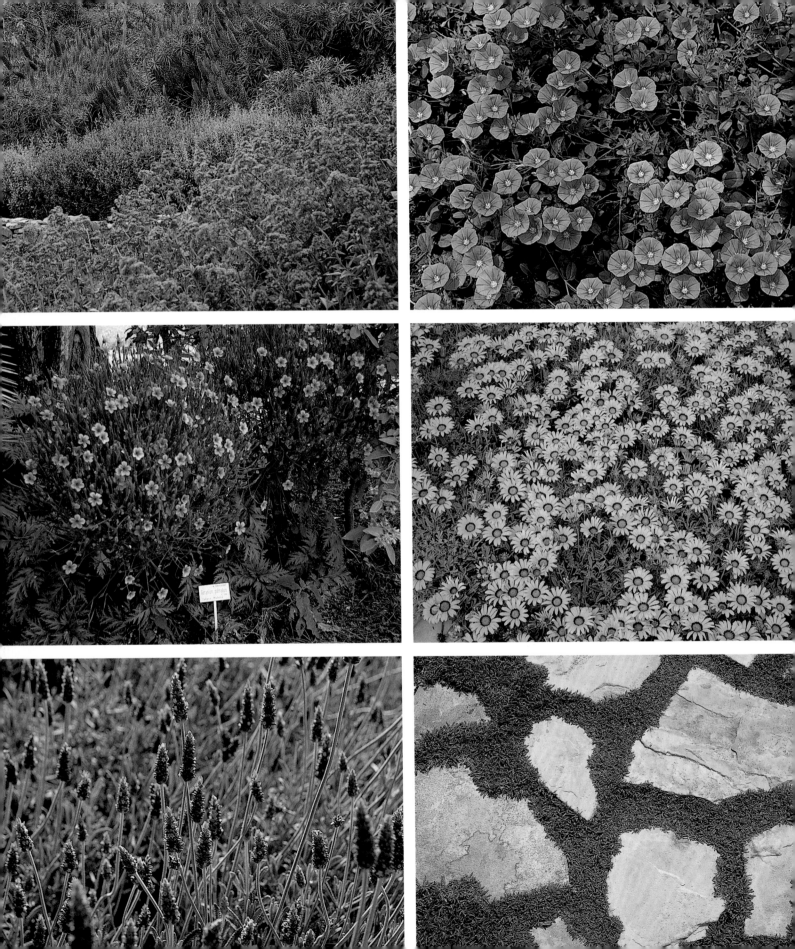

◀ Clockwise from top left: Jupiter's beard *(Centranthus rubra)* and pride of Madeira *(Echium candicans)*; Ground morning glory *(Convolvulus sabatius)*; Gazania rigens leucolaena hybrid; *Dymondia margaretae*; French, or toothed, lavender *(Lavandula dentata)*; *Geranium maderense*

▶ A mixed border, mediterranean style, is folded into the edge of an existing olive grove. The silvery tones of bush germander *(Teucrium fruticans)*, *Cistus* species, and dusty miller *(Senecio cineraria)* are accented by the bold, spiny foliage and upright stalks of the thistle-like biennial *Onopordum acanthium*.

▶ A simple but striking composition at the entrance to this mediterranean style garden in California demonstrates an effective use of drought-tolerant plants to soften architecture in a rarely irrigated area. Star jasmine *(Trachelospermum jasminoides)* clambers up the stone walls and will soon spill over the top. Potted dwarf olives *(Olea europaea* 'Little Ollie'*)* announce the garden's theme. A fruitless olive variety, 'Little Ollie' can be trained smaller than its usual dense, shrublike six feet by clipping or shearing, making it a boon to small gardens.

◀ Late winter, when barely colored spikes begin to emerge from mounds of gray-green foliage, is the time when everyone takes notice of pride of Madeira *(Echium candicans)*. These spirelike blooms elongate and turn jewel colors ranging from amethyst to sapphire.

▼ Many members of the great sage family can enhance the dry, sun-drenched garden. Among the best is Canary Island sage *(Salvia canariensis)*, with its six-foot arching canes covered in white woolly fuzz, and large, soft mauve clusters that appear to last from spring through summer because of their darker, persistent calyxes. A good background plant, it can shelter smaller plants and adapts to lack of summer water by not growing so tall.

▲ Silver and purple make a good palette for a mediterranean garden because there are so many plants to choose from in those colors. Backed by the feathery foliage of artemisia *(Artemisia arborescens)*, the trident bloom spikes of fernleaf lavender *(Lavandula multifida)* are emphasized by the larger composite blooms of verbena *(Verbena rigida)*. The silvery grass, *Festuca glauca* 'Elijah Blue', ties the group together. Tiny white flowers of snow in summer *(Cerastium tomentosum)* foam around and between. The whole planting survives on sparse and erratic irrigation throughout the summer.

◀ Stepping from stone to stone, one brushes through the aromatic foliage of lavender cotton *(Santolina chamaecyparissus)*. This Mediterranean native thrives in poor soil with little to no water, and can be sheared or left to bloom naturally.

▲ Moroccan wrought-iron gates and an old mission bell welcome visitors to this California garden, containing a collection of agaves, opuntias, and low-growing succulents, as well as a rare, variegated *Euphorbia ingens* behind the bell.

◀ Colorful and easy to care for, a choice mediterranean plant combination features strongly scented Copper Canyon daisy *(Tagetes lemmonii)* behind the clustered yellow blooms of dusty miller *(Senecio cineraria)*, and soft purple Cedros Island verbena *(Verbena lilacina)* in the foreground. Self-seeding nasturtiums, ranging from yellow to orange, twine through in the cool season and die out with summer heat.

INDEX

Page numbers in *italics* indicate
  illustrations.

A

acanthus, *167*
Aeonium species, 148, *154*
African boxwood, *98–99*, 100, *104–5*, 148
African daisy, *14–15, 160–61*
agave, *18–19, 111–13*, 148, *154, 171*
ageratum, 95
Aleppo pine, *66–67*
Alfarràs, Marquises of, *84*
Alhambra (Spain), *84*
aloe, 18, *39*, 148, *150–51, 154, 155*
alyssum, 95
American Academy, Rome (Italy), *18–19*
ancient gardens, 10–12, 14, 41, 42, 44,
  45, 71, 72, 87, 100, *134*
Andalusian style, *31, 84, 96–97*
Anduze pots, *136, 141–43*
aqueducts, 45, *91*
arbors, arches, and arcades, 12, 41, *49,
  51, 55, 84, 90, 99, 110, 121, 126, 145*
arborvitae, *46–47, 104–5*
Arctotis acaulis, 14–15, 160–61
aromatic plants, 8–10, 18, *29, 95*, 105,
  148
artemisia, 18, 148
artichokes, *121, 125*
asparagus, *94–95*, 105
aspidistra, *90*
asters, beach, 148
atriums, 72
Aurelia Hall, American Academy, Rome
  (Italy), *18–19*
Australia, 10, 14
Australian fuchsias, 100, *144–45*
Australian Garden, Lotusland
  (California), *144–45*
Australian tea trees, *144–45*
Australian willow, 95
automata, water-powered, *57, 80*
axiality, *32–33*, 100, *106, 116–17, 126,
  128–29, 136–37*
azulejo, 101, 144, 161

B

Ballota pseudodictamnus, 148
banksia roses, *24*
Barcelona (Spain), *53, 84, 91, 111, 139,
  140, 164*
Baroque gardens, *80, 90, 101, 116–17,
  138–39*
barrel cactus, *20, 69, 108–9, 155–59*
bastide farmhouses, *16–17, 25, 34–35,*
  77
bathing, outdoor, 74, 97
Baumgartner, Sydney, *144*
bay, 100, *122–23*
bay laurel (sweet bay), *28–29, 42,* 57
beach aster, 148
beans, *120, 122–23*
beaver tail cactus, *158–59*
begonias, *31*
black-eyed Susan vine, 97
book aloe, *155*
borders, mixed, 151, *167*
borrowed landscape, *24*
boschetti and *bosci,* 52
Boston ivy, *40–41,* 61, *76–77*
bougainvillea, 10, 18, *32–33, 152, 161*
box, *20–21, 32–33,* 49, *51, 56–57, 63,
  66–67, 86–87, 93–95, 98–99,* 100,
  *101, 104–7, 110, 120, 136–37,
  141–43,* 148, *160–61*
breath of heaven, *121*
bromeliads, *154*
bronze vegetation, 148
buckthorn, Italian, 74, 100
buckwheat, California, 148
buffalo grass, *115*
bulbs, 10, *115*
bunny ears cactus, *158–59*
burgundy-colored vegetation, 148
bush germander, *20–21,* 100, *102, 167*
bush sage, Mexican, *160–61*

C

cabinet di roccaglia, 80
Cabris (France), *82–83*
cactus, *20, 69, 89, 108–9,* 148, *154–59*

calades, 131–35
California buckwheat, 148
California fuchsia, 18
California mediterranean style, 10, 12,
  14, *28–29,* 31, 42, 58, *64–65, 86–87,*
  92, *95–97, 144–45. see also* specific
  sites
calla lilies, *46–47*
callistemons, 18
Canary Island palms, *66–67, 152*
Canary Island sage, *169*
Can Sureda (Majorca), *89*
canyon live oak, 42
cape plumbago, *27*
capers, 105
Cap Roig Botanic Garden (Spain), *164*
Carmel creeper, *93*
Caruncho, Fernando, *51*
Casa del Herrero (California), *62–65,
  84, 88–89, 120, 139, 144*
La Casa Pacifica (California), *31, 92, 152*
La Casella (France), *20–21, 27, 37,
  46–47, 89, 106, 107, 131–33*
casini, 128–29. see also pavilions
cast-iron plant, *90*
catena d'aqua, 59
caves, 72. *see also* grottoes
Ceanothus species, 147
cedar, 8
Cedric Island verbena, *170–71*
chahar bagh, 45
Château Ansouis (France), *106, 136*
Château Brantes (France), *40–41, 85*
Château Le Vignole, *34–35, 55, 102–3,
  141–43*
Château Val Joanis (France), *82, 120*
chestnut, 42
chiaroscuro effects, *108–9*
Chile, 10, 14
Chinese holly, *104–5*
Chiruchi, Thomas, 57
chives, 75
cistus (rockrose), 18, *28–29, 82–83,
  152–53, 167*
citrus, 8, 14, *18–19,* 23, *32–33, 46–47,*

  81, 98–99, 116–17, 124, 129–31, 164
classical mythology, *32–33, 42–43,* 47,
  57, 72, *78–79, 81, 84, 118*
clay, 12, *101–4,* 151
Cleveland sage, 18
climate, 10, 14, 147–51
climbing roses, *30,* 49
clipped greenery, *12, 13, 32–33, 37–39,
  46–47,* 49, *56–57,* 74, *82, 84,* 100,
  101–11, 114–17, 120, 129, 136–37,
  148
Clos du Peyronnet (France), *13, 30, 51,
  68–69, 126*
coast live oak, 42
coast rosemary (westringia), *95,* 100, 148,
  161
coffeeberry, 100
Cohen, Gil, *44, 129*
color, 8, *10,* 12, 14, 17–18, *20,* 25, *29, 45,*
  49, *51, 55,* 66, 74, *80, 82,* 100, *102,
  115, 122–23, 136–39,* 147–48, 151,
  152–53, 160–61, 169
containers. *see* pots and urns
Copper Canyon daisy, 18, *170–71*
correa, 18, 100, *144–45,* 148
Cotton, H. Hamilton, *92*
Cotyledon undulata, 148
courtyards, 18, *31, 63, 72–73, 86–87,* 90,
  161
crassulas, 148
crayfish, *49, 59*
creepers, *40–41,* 74, 77, *93, 98–99*
creeping fig, *84,* 95
creeping thyme, *16–17,* 95
Crete, 12
crowns, bay laurel, 57
cubism, *32*
culture, 10, 11, 14
cup-of-gold vine, *163*
cupolas, *32–33*
cushion bush, 148
cypress, 8, *12, 13, 16–17,* 18, *20–21,* 24,
  32– 35, 56–57, 72–73, 75, 77, *84,
  86–87, 89, 93,* 100, *102–6, 111, 120,
  129, 131, 164*

D

dates and date palms, 14, *53*
Delphi, 57
delphiniums, 151
details and elements, *98–145. see also* specific items
Domaine du Vignole, Le, *34–35, 55, 102–3, 141–43*
drought-resistant plantings, *24, 25, 31–33, 45, 55, 60, 76–77, 85, 118, 136, 147–51, 161, 167, 169*
Drucker, Bruce and Regina, *76–77*
dry gardens, 11, *20, 69, 147, 155–56, 161*
Dudleya brittonii, 148
dusty miller, *152–53, 167, 170–71*
dwarf plants, *20–21, 126, 155, 167*
Dyckia fosteriana, 154
Dymondia species, *28–29, 63, 166–67*

E

echeveria, 148, *154*
Egypt, 10, 41, 72
elements and details, *98–145. see also* specific items
empress trees, *130–31*
enclosed gardens, 11, 71, 72–74, 75, *82, 87, 120, 122–23*
Engelmann oak, 42
English laurel, *104–5*
English-style elements, *12, 49, 77, 101,* 151
English yew, *12, 104–5*
espaliering, *76–77, 102, 120, 144–45*
euphorbias, *108–9,* 148, *152, 159–61, 171*
Eureka lemons, *124, 161*
evening primrose, Mexican, *160–61*
evergreen (live) oaks, 42, *52*
evergreen trees, 42
exedra, 144

F

false sea onion, *161*
fennel, 105
fern asparagus, *94–95*
fernleaf lavender, *169*
Festuca glauca, 169
figs, 14, *84, 95*
fireplaces, outdoor, 74, *92, 95*
flag, yellow, *63*

Flanders field poppies, *12*
flannel bush, 18, *27*
flax, New Zealand, *31*
fleur de lis, 148–49
Florentine iris, *148–49*
Fontainebleau (France), *21*
Fontana, Carlo, *116, 126*
food and dining, 14, *23, 32–33, 40–41, 74, 76–77, 82,* 100, *104–5, 118–25,* 151
fountain grass, 148
fountains. *see* water elements
fragrance, 8–10, 18, *29, 95, 105,* 148
fraise du bois, 92
Fréjus (France), *36*
French lavender, *166–67*
French mediterranean style, *20–21, 24, 25, 29, 40–41, 49, 52, 70–71, 82, 93,* 104, *118–20, 140. see also* specific sites
fuchsia, 18, 100, *144–45*
Fundación Yannick y Ben Jakober (Majorca), *22–23*
furniture in the garden, *20, 25, 32–33, 52, 70–71, 74–76, 82–83, 85, 91–97, 136*

G

Gambera, Cardinal, *49, 59*
gates, *28–29, 39, 88–89,* 99, *120–22, 141, 152, 167, 171*
Gaudí, Antonio, *91*
Gazania rigens leucolaena hybrid, *166–67*
Generalife, Granada (Spain), *60*
geraniums, *24, 130–31, 139, 141–43*
germander, *20–21, 29,* 100, *102, 167*
Gervais, Paul, *44, 129*
giocci d'acqua (water jokes), *57, 80*
gods and goddesses, *32–33, 42–43, 47, 57, 72, 78–79, 81, 84, 118*
gourds, 41
grapes and grapevines, 14, *23, 52, 82–83, 136,* 148
grasses, *24, 77, 82–83, 97, 115, 148,* 151, *169*
Greece, 11, 12, *57,* 72, 100, 104, *134*
grid patterns, 42, 45, *61*
grottoes, *42–45,* 72, *78–79, 81*

ground morning glory, *166–67*
Guëll Park (Spain), *91*

H

Hanbury, Lady Dorothy, *141*
Hanbury Botanical Garden (Italy), *141*
hanging gardens, *126–27*
hawthornias, 148
hedges, *56–57,* 74, *84, 86–87, 89, 92,* 100, *106, 109, 120, 129,* 148
Heinsheimer, Julie, *82*
heliotrope, 151
Herbert, Gavin and Ninetta, *31*
herbs, 75, *104–5, 120, 122–23, 125,* 148. *see also* specific herbs
hermitages, *126*
Hidcote (England), 77
Hinoki false cypress, *104–5*
history, 10
holly, *104–5, 128–29*
holly oaks, *52*
Holm oak, 42
hop bush, *49, 66–67,* 74, *121,* 148, *160–61*
horse chestnut, 42
hortus, 14, *104–5*
hortus conclusus, 87
humanism, *106*
hummocky plants, 148
hydrangeas, *80*

I

iceberg roses, *95*
ice plant, 11, *32, 69*
impatiens, *31*
indusium, 17
iris, *30, 50, 82, 126, 148–49*
ironwork, 14, *20, 52, 82, 88–89, 97,* 104, *120, 138–41, 171*
irrigation and watering, *24, 25, 31–33, 45, 55, 60, 76–77, 85, 118, 136, 147–51, 161, 167, 169*
Islamic/Moorish style, 11–12, 14, *22–23,* 42, 45, *58, 60–66, 84, 89, 91,* 100, 101, *144, 171*
Italian buckthorn, 74, 100
Italian cypress, *13, 16–17, 20–21, 24, 34–35, 56–57, 72–73, 77, 86–87, 93, 102–3, 106, 120, 131, 164*

Italian mediterranean style, 11, *28–29, 38–39, 81, 86–87. see also* specific sites
ivy, *40–41, 61, 76–77, 94–95*
ivy geranium, *24, 139, 141–43*

J

jade plant, *155*
Jakober, Fundación Yannick y Ben (Majorca), *22–23*
Japanese box, *20–21, 63, 66, 160–61*
Japanese wisteria, *27*
Jardin Exotique (Monaco), *69*
Jas Crema (France), *20, 24, 26–27, 49, 65, 75, 77, 102*
jasmine, *51, 70–73, 167*
Johnston, Lawrence, 77
Judas tree, *108*
juniper, *66–67*
Jupiter's beard, *166–67*

K

kalanchoe, *155*
kale, 105
kitchen gardens, 14, *104–5, 118–25*
kohuhu, New Zealand, *108*
Korean grass, 97

L

Labertino d'Horta (Spain), El, *53, 84, 111*
labyrinths, *84, 106, 111*
Laguna Beach (California), *95*
Lambton, Lord, *12, 101*
Landriana (Italy), La, *54–55, 98–99, 152–53*
lantana, 18
latifolia, *56–57*
laurel, *28–29,* 42, 57, 100, *104–5*
lavender, 8, 18, *26–27, 61, 106, 120, 122, 146–47,* 148, *164–67, 169*
lavender cotton (santolina), 18, *29, 32–35, 89,* 100, *110, 129, 141–43,* 148, *152–53, 160–61, 168–69*
"lavendin," *122, 164–65*
lawns and grasses, *24, 77, 82–83, 97, 115,* 148, 151, *169*
lemons, *23, 116–17, 124, 129–31,* 164
lemon-scented thyme, *14–15*
lentisc, *82,* 147

licorice plant, *134*

lime trees (plane trees), *40–41, 42, 55, 61, 77, 128–29*

linden trees, *20, 42, 77*

lion's tail, 18

live oak, *42, 52*

living outdoors, 10–11, *31, 70–97*

locust trees, *76–77*

loggias, 12, *49, 90*

loquat, 77

Lotusland (California), *20, 58, 108–9, 111–13, 124, 144–45, 155–57*

lovage, *120*

Luma apiculata, 104–5

luminescent vegetation, 17–18, 147–48

M

Majorca, *22–23, 39, 51, 60, 66, 89*

Manship, Paul, *72*

maples, *98–99*

Marimurta Botanical Garden (Spain), *32–33*

Martin, George, *97*

Mas Oiseau (France), *140*

mastic, 147

Matisse Museum (France), *35*

mazes, *84, 106, 111*

McDuffie, Mr. & Mrs. Malcolm, *61*

McElwee, Carole, *17, 66–67, 87, 160–61*

McKim, Mead, and White, *72*

meadow gardens, *115*

Medici family, *9, 50, 115, 126, 126–27, 130–31, 131*

Mesopotamia, 10

Mexican bush sage, *160–61*

Mexican daisy, *134*

Mexican evening primrose, *160–61*

Mexican gem, *154*

Mexican plumeria, *144*

Michelozzi, Michelozzo, 9, *126–27*

mint, *75*

mixed borders, 151, *167*

modernism, *51, 140*

Monaco, *69*

moneywort, *98–99*

Moore, Wally and Susie, *17, 75*

Moorish/Islamic style, 11–12, 14, *22–23, 42, 45, 58, 60–66, 84, 89, 91, 100, 101, 144, 171*

morning glory, *166–67*

Morocco, 45

Mortola (Italy), La, *141*

mosaic, 100–101, *131–35*

mounded plant shapes, 148

mulberry trees, *42, 85*

Mus, Jean, *34–35, 55, 82, 102, 141*

musical water cascade, *59*

mustard, 105

myrtle, *14–15,* 18, 100, *104–5,* 147

mythological figures, *32–33, 42–43, 47, 57,* 72, *78–79, 81, 84,* 118

N

nasturtiums, *121, 170–71*

nepeta, 18

New Zealand flax, *31*

New Zealand kohuhu, *108*

Nixon, Richard, *31, 92*

Noailles, Charles Viscount de, *32, 77, 110, 115*

Norway maples, *98–99*

nymphaea, 72, *81. see also* grottoes

O

oaks, *42, 52, 128–29*

oleanders, *81*

olive oil, *118, 138–39*

olive trees, 8, 14, *24, 26–29, 35, 37, 42, 49, 54–55, 61, 75, 77, 82–83, 86–87, 115, 118,* 131, 147, *152–53, 164–65, 167*

Onopordum acanthium, 167

opuntias, *171*

orange garden, La Landriana (Italy), *81, 98–99*

orchi, 118

oriental arborvitae, *104–5*

orris, *148–49*

outdoor living, 10–11, *31, 70–97*

P

Pacific wax myrtle, *14–15,* 100, 147

Page, Russell, *99*

painting, *78,* 104

palissades, 56–57, 84

palm trees, *53, 66–67, 152*

pansies, *95*

paradise gardens, 11–12, *42–45, 60, 63*

parsley, 105

parsnips, 105

parterres, *56–57, 106–7*

Pasadena (California), *76–77*

paths and walkways, *16–17, 24, 28–29, 32–33, 49,* 99, *115, 126, 152–53, 168–69*

patios, *51, 60, 64–66, 84, 88–90, 92, 95–97, 99, 144*

pavilions, *32–33, 48–49, 77, 78, 111, 128–29*

paving, 14, *16–17, 20–21, 24, 27, 28–29, 31, 35, 72–73, 75, 77, 82–83, 85–87,* 99–101, *122–23, 131–36, 144–45*

pebble mosaic, 100–101, *131–35*

pelargonium, *24, 56–57, 75, 139, 141–43*

pepper trees, *11,* 42

pergolas, 12, 14, *24, 30, 41, 44, 50,* 99, *120, 124, 131–33*

peristyles, arcades, arbors, and arches, 12, *41, 49, 51, 55, 84, 90,* 99, *110, 121, 126, 145*

Persia, 11, 14, 41, 42

Persian Wheel, 45

perspectives and views, *9, 20, 24, 30, 32, 38–39, 87–89, 91, 98–99, 106, 116–17, 126–31, 136, 138–39, 144–45*

Phillyria latifolia, 56–57

philosophy, 10, 11, 14, 100, *106*

pianelle, 24, 50

pietra dura, 80, 81

pine, 8, *22, 66–67*

Pinsent, Cecil, *39, 52, 78, 81, 87,* 115

Pittosporum tenuifolium, 100, *108–9*

plane trees (lime trees), *40–41, 42, 55, 61, 77, 128–29*

plants and plantings, *146–71. see also* individual plants

Plectranthus argentatus, 144–45, 148

Pliny the Younger, *41,* 42, *71*

plumbago, *27*

plumeria, Mexican, *144*

pollarding, 27, *40–41, 55,* 85

pomegranates, 14, 18, *23,* 120, *125*

Pomme d'Ambre (France), La, *36*

Pompadour, Madame, *21*

Pompeii, 45

ponds and pools. *see* water elements

poppies, *12*

Portugal, 100

Portugal laurel, *104–5*

*potagers (*kitchen gardens), 14, *104–5, 118–25*

potpourri, *125*

pots and urns, 12, *18–19, 22–23, 25, 36, 38, 61, 66–67, 75–77, 80, 81, 88–89, 92, 93, 95, 106, 118, 122–23, 129, 130–31, 134, 136–37, 141–43, 155, 161*

pride of Madeira, *28–29, 166–67, 169*

primrose, *160–61*

prostrate rosemary, *49, 164–65*

provençal gardens. *see* French mediterranean style

purple vegetation, 148

Q

quadripartite gardens, 11–12, *42–45, 86–87, 106, 120*

queen's wreath, *163*

R

Rabinovich, Jacob and Gina, *28–29, 49*

ramada, 96–97

rambling roses, *25*

religion, 10, 11, 14, 100, *106. see also* Islamic/Moorish style; paradise gardens

Renaissance gardens, *9,* 12, *32–33, 38–39, 42–43, 45, 48–50, 52, 56–57, 59,* 72, *78–81, 106–7, 114–15, 128–31*

retaining walls, *20, 82–83, 104–5, 126–27*

ribat, 22–23, 65

Riviera, 45, *82, 126, 141*

rockrose (cistus), 18, *28–29, 82–83, 152–53, 167*

rocks and stones, 8, 18, *39, 69,* 151, *168–69*

Roger's Gardens, *152*

Rome, ancient, 12, 14, 41, 71, 72, *91, 104–5*

rosemary, *16–17,* 18, *23, 27–29, 49, 82, 95,* 100, *101, 160–61, 164–65*

roses, *23–27, 30, 41, 49, 50, 70–71, 75,*

82–83, 95, 99, 106, 120, 148, 151
Roussillon (France), 136
rue, 105

S

sage, 8, 18, 75, 160–61, 169
saguaro, 155–57
salvia, 160–61
samphire, 105
San Clemente (California), 31
sandhill sage, 18
sandpaper vine, 163
San Juan Capistrano (California), 16–17, 25
Santa Barbara (California), 20, 58, 61–65, 84, 88–89, 93, 108–9, 111–13, 120, 124, 144–45, 155–57
santolina (lavender cotton), 18, 29, 32–35, 89, 100, 110, 129, 141–43, 148, 152–53, 160–61, 168–69
scent, 8–10, 18, 29, 95, 105, 148
Schienert, Claus, 21
Scott, Geoffrey, 39, 52, 87
sculpture, 18, 40, 42–45, 47, 57, 66–67, 72, 78–79, 84, 97, 116–17, 141
seasons, 10, 115
sedum, 155
sempervirens roses, 23
sempervivum, 148
shade and sunshine, 10, 12, 18, 20, 27, 32–33, 39, 41–45, 48–57, 61, 77, 82, 85, 128–29
shell decorations, 72, 81, 94–95
showers, outdoor, 74, 97
shrimp plant, 151
Smith, George Washington, 84
smoke bush, 148
snow in summer, 169
soap aloe, 154
sotto conche, 131
sour oranges, 98–99
South Africa, 10, 14
Spanish mediterranean style, 11, 14, 31, 45, 51, 58, 60–65, 84, 89, 92, 96–97, 100, 104, 139, 144. see also specific sites
spear lily, 144–45
sphinx, 47

springs. see water elements
spugna, 72, 78, 81
squash, 125
St. Fiacre, 66–67
staircases and steps, 27–28, 31, 36, 77, 89, 101, 126, 138–39, 141–44
star creeper, 98–99
star jasmine, 72–73, 167
star-shaped pools, 58, 64–65
statuary, 18, 40, 42–45, 47, 57, 66–67, 72, 78–79, 84, 97, 116–17, 141
Steedman, Mr. & Mrs. George Fox, 65, 84, 89, 139
Stevens, Ralph, 65
stones and rocks, 8, 18, 39, 69, 151, 168–69
strawberries, 92, 125
Strong, Charles Augustus, 78
succulents, 148, 154, 155, 171
sunflowers, 23
sunken gardens, 110
sunshine and shade, 10, 12, 18, 20, 27, 32–33, 39, 41–45, 48–57, 61, 77, 82, 85, 128–29
Sutera cordata, 95
sweet alyssum, 95
sweet bay (bay laurel), 28–29, 42, 57
swimming pools, 66–67
symmetry, 32–33, 100, 106, 116–17, 126, 128–29, 136–37
sisyrinchium, 27

T

tarragon, 75
Taverna, Lavinia, 99
tea trees, 144–45
terracing, 9, 14–15, 26–27, 32–33, 36, 37, 50, 51, 66–69, 79, 82–83, 89, 99, 106, 115, 126–27, 128–31
terra cotta, 12, 29, 77, 80, 101–4, 118, 129
tèse, 49
texture, 13, 17–18, 66, 151, 161
thyme, 14–15, 16–17, 75, 95
tile, 14, 58, 61–66, 88–89, 91, 101, 140, 144, 161
tobira, 89, 104–5, 152
tomatoes, 121, 122–23

tondo, 18–19, 116–17, 131
toothed lavender, 166–67
topiary. see clipped greenery
training plants, 12, 14, 24, 30, 41, 44, 50–52, 76–77, 82–83, 99, 102, 120, 124, 131–33, 140, 144–45
trellises, 14, 51, 52, 82–83
tuteur, 121

U

upright rosemary, 16–17
urns. see pots and urns

V

valerian, 29
Valle Pinciole (Italy), 104–5
van Gogh iris, 148–49
variegated greenery, 11, 95, 100, 108, 154, 171
Verbascum species, 148
verbena, 160–61, 170–71
vessels. see pots and urns
viale, 129
Victorian era, 45
views and vistas, 9, 20, 24, 30, 32, 38–39, 87–89, 91, 98–99, 106, 116–17, 126–31, 136, 138–39, 144–45
Vignola, Giacomo Barozzi da, 59, 129
Vignole, Le Domaine/Château du, 34–35, 55, 102–3, 141–43
Villa Aurelia, American Academy, Rome, 18–19, 57, 72–73, 138–39
Villa Chigi Cetinale (Italy), 12, 101, 116–17, 126
Villa di Geggiano (Italy), 78, 131
Villa Gamberaia (Italy), 56–57, 80, 81
Villa Lante (Italy), 32–33, 42–43, 48–49, 57, 59, 78, 128–29
Villa le Balze (Italy), 38–39, 52, 78–79, 81, 87, 114–15, 136–37
Villa Massai (Italy), 44, 45, 129, 140
Villa Medici (Italy), 9, 50, 115, 126–27, 130–31
Villa Noailles (France), 77, 110, 115
vinca, 95
vines, 8, 14, 34–35, 40–41, 51, 82–84, 93–95, 97, 126–27, 140, 161, 163. see also specific types

Virginia creeper, 40–41, 74, 77
visual elements, 17–18
vittidinia, 134

W

Waldner, Lulu de, 20, 49, 75
walkways and paths, 16–17, 24, 28–29, 32–33, 49, 99, 115, 126, 152–53, 168–69
walled gardens, 11, 71, 72–74, 75, 82, 87, 120, 122–23
Walska, Ganna, 108
water effects, dry designs emulating, 69, 161
water elements, 11, 14–15, 18, 20–21, 30, 32–33, 40–49, 56–69, 72–73, 78–80, 84, 86–87, 106, 111, 128–29
Waterfield, William, 30
water hyacinth, 46–47
watering and irrigation, 24, 25, 31–33, 45, 55, 60, 76–77, 85, 118, 136, 147–51, 161, 167, 169
water iris, 21–22, 46–47, 63
water lilies, 30, 46–47, 56–57, 63
Watterson, Jim, 97
wattle fencing, 104–5
wellheads, reclaimed, 65
"The Western White House" (La Casa Pacifica), 31, 92, 152
westringia (coast rosemary), 95, 100, 148, 161
whitewashing tree trunks, 124
Whitney, Lew, 152
wildflowers, 10, 115
willow, 95
wire vine, 140, 161
wisteria, 27, 51, 75, 96–97, 162–63
woolly blue curls, 18
wrought iron, 14, 20, 52, 82, 88–89, 97, 104, 120, 138–41, 171

Y

yellow flag, 63
yew, 12, 34–35, 56–57, 82, 100, 104–5, 120, 129
yucca, 31, 111–13, 148

FEATURED GARDENS THAT MAY BE VISITED BY APPOINTMENT

Most of the photographs found in *Sun-Drenched Gardens: The Mediterranean Style* were made while traveling under the magnificent guidance of Ingatours. Inga Stone, a qualified guide with more than fifteen years experience in the field, leads small groups to visit selected gardens as if on a private tour, but without the worry. We found her assistance and enthusiasm for our gardening interests to be invaluable and trust you will too. More information on Ingatours is available at www.ingatours.com or by direct phone contact at: (U.S.) 800–581–0911 or (U.K.) 44–20–8868–0543.

Should you wish to make your own travel arrangements, the gardens below may be contacted to schedule a visit. Enjoy!

FRANCE

La Casella
23 Chemin du Molin
Opio, 06130 Grasse, France
Claus Scheinert

Château d'Ansouis
84240 Ansouis, France

Château Brantes
84700 Sorgues, France

Château Val Joanis
84120 Pertuis, France
tel. 33–04–90–79–20–77
fax 33–04–90–09–69–52

Clos du Peyronnet
Avenue Aristide Briand
06500 Menton, France
William Waterfield
tel. 33–04–93–35–72–15
fax 33–04–93–35–72–25

ITALY

American Academy in Rome
Via Angelo Masina 5
00153 Rome, Italy
tel. 39–06–584–6444

La Landriana
Via Campo di Carne 51
00040 Tor San Lorenzo
Ardea (Rome), Italy
tel. 39–06–910–14140
fax 39–06–687–2839

Villa le Balze
Via Vecchia Fiesolana 26
50014 Fiesole (Florence), Italy
The Charles Augustus Strong Center of Georgetown University

Villa Chigi Cetinale
Sovicille
53018 Sienna, Italy

Villa Gamberaia
Via del Rossellino 72
50135 Settignano (Florence), Italy
Anne Pellegrini
tel. 39–055–697–205
fax 39–055–697–027

Villa Lante
(public garden)
Viterbo, Italy

Villa Massei
55060 Massa Macinaia
Lucca, Italy
Gil Cohen or Paul Gervais
fax 39–05–839–0138
www.agardeninlucca.com

SPAIN

Cap Roig Botanic Garden
(public garden)
Calella de Palafrugell, Spain

Güell Park
(public garden)
Barcelona, Spain

El Laberinto d'Horta
(public garden)
Barcelona, Spain

Marimurta Botanic Garden
Calella de Palafrugell, Spain

UNITED STATES

Casa del Herrero
1387 East Valley Road
Montecito, CA 93108
Diane Galt
tel. 805–565–5653

Ganna Walska Lotusland
695 Ashley Road
Montecito, CA 93108
Steven Timbrook
tel. 805–969–9990

SUGGESTED READING AND REFERENCE

Bajard, Sophie, and Raffaello Benecini. *Villas and Gardens of Tuscany.* Paris: Pierre Terrail, 1994.

Citron, Joan, ed. *Selected Plants for Southern California Gardens.* Los Angeles: Southern California Horticultural Society, 2000.

Clebsch, Betsy. *A Book of Salvias.* Portland, OR: Timber Press, 1997.

Creasy, Rosalind. *The Complete Book of Edible Landscaping.* San Francisco: Sierra Club Books, 1982.

Dallman, Peter R. *Plant Life in the World's Mediterranean Climates.* Sacramento: California Native Plant Society, 1998.

Farrar, Linda. *Ancient Roman Gardens.* Phoenix Mill, Gloucestershire, UK: Sutton Publishing, 1998.

Gervais, Paul. *A Garden in Lucca.* New York: Hyperion, 2000.

Gildemeister, Heidi. *Mediterranean Gardening: A Waterwise Approach.* Palma de Majorca, Spain: Editoral Moll, 1995.

Harbouri, Carolyn, ed. *The Mediterranean Garden Journal.* Peania, Greece: The Mediterranean Garden Society, 1995–.

Howarth, Maggy. *The Art of Pebble Mosaics: Creative Designs and Techniques for Paths and Patios.* Turnbridge Wells, Kent, UK: Search Press Ltd., 1994.

Jellicoe, Goode & Landcaster. *The Oxford Companion to Gardens.* Oxford, UK: Oxford University Press, 1986.

Jones, Louisa. *Gardens in Provence.* Paris: Flammarion, 1992.

Kourik, Robert. *The Lavender Garden.* San Francisco: Chronicle, 1998.

Latymer, Hugo. *The Mediterranean Gardener.* London: Frances Lincoln Ltd., 1990.

Leszczynski, Nancy A. *Planting the Landscape: A Professional Approach to Landscape.* New York: John Wiley & Sons, 1999.

Mathias, Mildred E. *Color for the Landscape.* Arcadia, CA: California Arboretum Foundation, 1976.

Noailles, Charles Viscount de, and Roy Landcaster. *Mediterranean Plants and Gardens.* Calverton, Nottingham, UK: Floraprint Ltd., 1977.

Nottle, Trevor. *Gardens of the Sun.* Portland, OR: Timber Press, 1997.

Perry, Bob. *Landscape Plants for Western Regions.* Claremont, CA: Land Design Publishing, 1992.

Power, Nancy Goslee. *The Gardens of California.* New York: Clarkson Potter, 1995.

Quest-Ritson, Charles. *The English Garden Abroad.* London: Penguin Books, 1996.

Taverna, Lavinia. *La Compagnia di un Giardino.* Grosseto, Italy: Tipografia Ombrone, 1997.

Western Garden Book. Menlo Park, CA: Lane Publishing, 2001.

Wharton, Edith. *Italian Villas and Their Gardens.* New York: The Century Company, 1904.